D0839452

Taxation of Americans in Canada

Dale Walters, CPA, PFS, CFP®
with Sally Taylor, CPA, and David Levine, CA, CPA

Self-Counsel Press
(a division of)
International Self-Counsel Press Ltd.
USA   Canada

Self-Counsel Press acknowledges the financial support of the Government of Canada through the Canada Book Fund (CBF) for our publishing activities.

Printed in Canada.

First edition: 2016

Library and Archives Canada Cataloguing in Publication

Walters, Dale, 1958-, author
     Taxation of Americans in Canada : are you at risk? / Dale Walters, CPA, PFS, CFP® ; with Sally Taylor, CPA, and David Levine, CA, CPA.

Issued in print and electronic formats.

ISBN 978-1-77040-147-1 (paperback).—ISBN 978-1-77040-874-6 (epub).—ISBN 978-1-77040-875-3 (kindle)

     1. Americans—Canada—Finance, Personal. 2. Americans—Taxation—Law and legislation—Canada. 3. Americans—Legal status, laws, etc.—Canada. 4. Income tax—Law and legislation—United States. I. Taylor, Sally, author II. Levine, David, author III. Title.

HG179.W33 2016   332.024'008913071   C2016-901703-6
                                                    C2016-901704-4

MIX
Paper from
responsible sources
FSC
www.fsc.org   FSC® C004071

Self-Counsel Press
(a division of)
International Self-Counsel Press Ltd.

Bellingham, WA   North Vancouver, BC
       USA   Canada

Contents

3 An Overview of Canadian Taxation

4   The Treaty   52

5   Foreign Tax Credits   64

6   Retirement Plans, Pensions, and Social Security   71

12 Americans in Noncompliance with the IRS 171

Resources

Tables

Notice to Readers

Laws are constantly changing. Every effort is made to keep this publication as current as possible. However, the author, the publisher, and the vendor of this book make no representations or warranties regarding the outcome or the use to which the information in this book is put and are not assuming any liability for any claims, losses, or damages arising out of the use of this book. The reader should not rely on the author or the publisher of this book for any professional advice. Please be sure that you have the most recent edition.

Prices, commissions, fees, and other costs mentioned in the text or shown in examples in this book may not reflect real costs where you live. Inflation and other factors, including geography, can cause the costs you might encounter to be much higher or even much lower than those we show. The dollar amounts shown are simply intended as representative examples.

Circular 230 Disclaimer: Nothing in this book is to be used or relied upon by anyone for the purposes of avoiding penalties that may be imposed on you under the Internal Revenue Code of 1986, as amended. Any statements contained within this book relating to any federal tax transaction or matter may not be used by any person to support the promotion or marketing to recommend any federal tax transaction. Everyone should seek advice based on individual circumstances from a qualified independent cross-border tax advisor. No one, without express written permission, may use any part of this book in promoting, marketing, or recommending an arrangement relating to any federal tax matter to anyone else.

Acknowledgments

Robert (Bob) Keats, saw a need for US-Canada financial planning, and has been serving Canadians and Americans with cross-border issues for more than 30 years. In 1990, he founded Keats, Connelly and Associates, which is now called KeatsConnelly. It is because of Bob's foresight and hard work that we are now able to write a book dedicated solely to the taxation of Americans in Canada.

We also want to acknowledge all of the KeatsConnelly employees, past and present, on their contributions to this book. This is the cumulative effort of decades of employees learning this subject matter by working directly with clients day after day, year after year. We have tried to capture their cumulative knowledge in this book.

Ultimately, if it were not for the support and understanding of our spouses we would not have been able to accomplish such a large undertaking as this. Because the time we spent researching, writing, and editing took away time from our families, their patience and encouragement to finish the book was essential.

This is the second book that the authors have collaborated on and the fifth in the Cross-Border Series. The success of these books is due entirely to people like you who buy and read our books. We have been told that some of you have read every book in the series. To you and all of the readers of these books, we sincerely say: Thank you!

Lastly, we want to thank all of the clients we have worked with over the years. It is our clients who have put us in a position to be able to write a book on this topic in the first place. Without them this book would not have been possible. It is for them and all future clients that we write this book.

1

Before You Go to Canada

Assuming you decide Canada is the right place for you and you're not already resident, before you move to Canada, you need do a lot of planning. Just moving across town you have to think about what to take and what to leave behind. You have to think about how to notify everyone of your new phone number and mailing address. You have to decide about packing and physically moving your belongings, and whether to do it yourself or hire a moving company.

When moving to a new country, the issues are exponentially more complex. You may think about immigration, applying for health insurance, and obtaining a tax ID number. Unfortunately, tax planning is typically ignored or postponed until it is too late.

1. Planning Your Move

Canada provides a number of good resources that will help with your move, but before you look at those resources you must consider the implications of leaving the US.

From a tax perspective, there are three broad categories that people fall into when leaving the US and each has different tax ramifications. The categories are US citizens, long-term permanent residents (green card holders), and anyone that is neither a US citizen nor a long-term green card holder. A long-term permanent resident is defined as a person who has been a "Lawful

Permanent Resident," also known as a green card holder, for at least 8 out of the last 15 years.

Note: The definition of a long-term resident is very precise and applies only to green card holders. Therefore you can be in the US for 10, 20, or more years using a Visa and you would never be considered a long-term permanent resident.

The easiest category from a tax perspective is that of US citizens that continue to retain their US citizenship when they move out of the US. As a US citizen, you simply need to do some tax planning before you move. We will talk about tax planning and expatriation later in this chapter.

If you are not a US citizen and are not a long-term green card holder, you are required to obtain a Certificate of Compliance, also known as a Sailing Permit, before leaving the US. To get a Certificate of Compliance, you must go to a local IRS office between two and four weeks before leaving the US. You must file either the Form 2063 tax statement (short form) or the Form 1040-C tax return (long form) and take it with you to an IRS office to obtain a Certificate of Compliance. The certificate cannot be issued more than 30 days before you leave. If you are married, you each must receive a clearance certificate; therefore you and your spouse must each file one of the forms and go to the IRS office.

Form 2063 is the short form that asks for some basic information, but does not compute the tax due. You are qualified to use the short form if you have filed a least one tax return (and paid tax, if applicable) in the US, and are an —

- individual who had no taxable income during the year up to the date of departure, or

- individual who had taxable income during the year or preceding year and "whose departure will not hinder the collection of any tax." If the IRS has information indicating that you are leaving to avoid paying tax, you must file Form 1040-C and pay the tax.

Examples of aliens not required to obtain a Certificate of Compliance are diplomats; students; those receiving no taxable income; and alien residents of Canada or Mexico who commute and have wages that are subject to withholding.

Important: We strongly recommend that you call two or more months ahead to schedule an appointment if you are filing one of these forms. It will likely be very difficult to find IRS agents who will know what to do when you call for an appointment since they likely don't encounter these forms on a daily basis. Calling ahead will give you and them time to find someone who knows what to do, or at least the opportunity to learn what to do.

2. Expatriation

US citizens and Lawful Permanent Residents (green card holders) are required to report and pay tax on their worldwide income, regardless of where they reside. To remove yourself from the US tax system, you must give up your citizenship or green card and become a nonresident alien. For US citizens to become nonresident aliens, they must renounce their citizenship and move to another country.

An expatriation tax applies to US citizens who renounce their citizenship and long-term residents who end their residency. A long-term resident is defined as someone who has been a green card holder for at least 8 of the 15 years prior to expatriation.

For those of you eligible to become US citizens who are deciding whether to become citizens before you leave, we would say that there are a lot of factors that must be considered and weighed before making that decision. Things to consider are:

- There is no income tax difference between a citizen and a long-term green card holder, before, during, or after expatriation.

- The advantages of citizenship over being a green card holder are:

  - Estate tax advantage: US citizens are allowed to receive unlimited assets from a spouse they are legally married to, without the deceased spouse paying US estate tax at his or her death.

  - The right to vote in US elections.

  - Protection or assistance by the US government and/or military when overseas.

  - The right to enter the US and stay as long as you desire.

The benefits green card holders have are —

- green cards are easier to give up than citizenship, if that time ever comes, and

- it is possible to relinquish and reacquire green card status, where it is nearly impossible to reacquire citizenship if it is surrendered.

2.1 Relinquishing US citizenship

You are considered to have relinquished your US citizenship on the earliest of the following dates:

1. The date you renounce your US citizenship before a diplomatic or consular officer of the US, assuming the renouncement was later confirmed by the issuance of a Certificate of Loss of Nationality (CLN).

2. The date the State Department issues a CLN.

3. The date a US court cancels your Certificate of Naturalization.

2.2 Relinquishing Lawful Permanent Resident status

A long-term resident terminates his or her residency on the earliest of the following dates:

1. The date he or she voluntarily abandons Lawful Permanent Resident status by filing Form I-407 with a US consular or immigration officer and they have determined that he or she has, in fact, abandoned Lawful Permanent Resident status.

2. The date he or she becomes subject to a final administrative order for removal from the US under the Immigration and Nationality Act, and actually leaves the US as a result of that order.

3. If he or she was a dual resident of the US and a country with which the US has an income tax treaty (such as Canada), the date he or she commences to be treated as a resident of that country and determines that, for purposes of the treaty, he or she is a resident of the treaty country and gives notice to the Secretary of such treatment.

Although a person who expatriates will be treated as a nonresident alien, he or she may be classified as a "covered expatriate," which would subject the person to an exit tax, similar to the tax Canada imposes on its residents when they leave Canada and become residents of other countries. The exit tax imposes an immediate tax, as well as potential future taxes on the expatriate. A covered expatriate is either a US citizen or long-term resident who abandons or loses his or her status as a US citizen or permanent resident, and as of the day before expatriation has:

1. Average net income tax for the last five years of more than $161,000 (2016), or

2. Net worth on the date of expatriation of $2 million or more, or

3. Failed to certify, under penalty of perjury, that he or she has complied with all US federal tax obligations for the five years preceding the date of expatriation or termination of residency. Certification is done using Form 8854 (more on this form later). This form is completed when filing Form 1040 (or 1040NR) for the year of expatriation.

The income tax amount of $161,000 is increased for cost-of-living adjustment each year. There is no adjustment for the net worth amount of $2 million. The $161,000 amount is the tax, not the income. This means that if you assume an average or effective tax rate of 30%, you need over $525,000 of taxable income (not gross income). This seems like a much higher threshold than $2 million net worth, so the vast majority of those expatriating will be considered a covered expatriate due to having a net worth in excess of $2 million.

If you expatriate and you are considered a covered expatriate, you will be subject to a "mark-to-market tax," also known as a deemed disposition of your worldwide assets, and will be required to recognize gain on those assets as if they were sold at their fair market value as of the day prior to your expatriation.

Note: If you are a long-term resident, you have the option to use the fair market value of your assets on the day your US residency began. For the assets you owned when you moved to the US, this will, in most cases, be a higher number and therefore produce a lower gain than using the original purchase price.

There are three groups of assets that are not subject to the mark-to-market tax, but will be taxed using a different method: 1) deferred compensation, 2) tax-deferred accounts, and 3) an interest in a non-grantor trust. If you have one or more of these types of accounts, you must file Form W-8CE within 30 days of expatriation.

Deferred compensation is divided into two types; one that has a US payor that is required to withhold on all payments, and one for all other deferred compensation arrangements. Where US withholding is required, payment can be deferred until payment is made, but the withholding must be 30%. The covered expatriate cannot claim, under the treaty, to reduce the withholding. For all other deferred compensation arrangements, the accrued benefit will be treated as being received the day before expatriation.

Examples of deferred compensation plans include a company pension or profit sharing plan (including 401(k) and 403(b) accounts), simplified employee pensions (SEP), and simplified retirement accounts (SIMPLE plans).

Any interests in a foreign pension or retirement account are considered deferred compensation plans and are included in the expatriation tax. This includes your RRSPs, RRIFs, LIRAs, any Canadian company pension, and government or military pension, but does not include Canadian Pension Plan or Old Age Security, which are forms of social security.

Tax-deferred accounts are individual retirement plans, a qualified tuition plan (aka Section 529 Plan), a Coverdell Education Savings Account, a health savings account, and an Archer MSA. However, Simplified Employee Pension (SEP) and SIMPLE IRA plans of a covered expatriate are treated as deferred compensation items described above. These plans are treated as if the entire interest was paid out on the day prior to expatriation.

The definition of a non-grantor trust is a trust that occurs when the grantor gives the control of the trust property to a trustee other than himself. In other words, a non-grantor trust is a trust that someone established for the benefit of someone other than himself or herself. So, if someone (your parent for example) established a trust in which you are the beneficiary, or at least one of the beneficiaries, the value of your share of the trust is subject to the expatriation tax. If you are the beneficiary of such a trust, the trustee must withhold 30% of any direct or indirect distributions. This withholding rule applies to both domestic (US) and foreign (non-US) trusts.

There are two exceptions from the automatic treatment of the tax described above. The first is for a dual citizen who became a US citizen at birth and must have also become a citizen of the other country at birth, or someone who was a resident of the US for 10 years or less, out of the last 15, prior to the year in which the expatriation occurred. This second exception refers to naturalized citizens (those who went through the process of becoming a US citizen).

The second exception is for certain minors, if (and only if) all of the following conditions are met —

- the minor became a US citizen at birth,
- expatriation occurs before attaining age 18, and
- the minor was not a US resident for more than ten years before expatriation occurs.

Important: If you are subject to the expatriate tax regime, the US provides an exemption from the tax on gains in excess of $693,000 (2016 and indexed for inflation). This means that many of you will not owe tax upon expatriating. If your gain is greater than $693,000, you pay tax on the difference.

Note: you can make an irrevocable election to defer the payment of the tax. If you make the election, the following rules apply:

1. You must make the election on a property-by-property basis.

2. The deferred tax on a particular property is due on the return for the tax year in which you dispose of the property.

3. You must provide adequate security, such as a bond.

4. Interest is charged for the period the tax is deferred.

5. The due date for the payment of the deferred tax cannot be extended beyond the earlier of the following dates:

   - The due date of the return required for the year of death.

   - The time that the security provided for the property fails to be adequate.

6. You must make an irrevocable waiver of any right under any treaty of the US that would preclude assessment or collection of any tax imposed under this expatriation regime.

7. You must file Form 8854 annually for each year, up to and including the year in which the full amount of deferred tax and interest is paid.

Important: The consequence of being in the US for more than 30 days, in any calendar year, after expatriation is that you will be treated as a US citizen for tax purposes and taxed on your worldwide income. This rule will apply for the longer of ten years or until the full amount of deferred tax and interest is paid. There is one exception to this rule. You can be in the US for up to 60 days without being treated as a US citizen if any of the following requirements are met:

- you were performing personal services in the US for an employer who is not related to you, and you meet these additional requirements;

- you were a US citizen and, within a reasonable period of time following your expatriation, you became a citizen or resident, fully liable to tax in the country in which you, your spouse, or either of your parents were born; or

- for each year, in the ten years prior to your expatriation, you were physically present in the US for 30 days or fewer.

Form 8854: Initial and Annual Expatriation Statement must be filed upon the date of renunciation with the American Citizen Services section of the nearest American Embassy or consulate. (See the Resources at the back of this book for a list of forms and where to find them as you read through this book.)

In addition to the information discussed in the preceding sections, the following information is required:

1. the taxpayer's identification number (Social Security number),

2. the mailing address of the principal foreign residence,

3. expatriation date,

4. the foreign country in which the individual is residing,

5. the foreign country or countries of which the individual is a citizen and the date he or she became a citizen of those foreign countries,

6. information detailing the income, assets, and liabilities of the individual,

7. the number of days during any portion of which the individual was physically present in the US during the taxable year, and

8. how he or she became a US citizen (birth or naturalization).

3. Your Rights after US Citizenship Is Terminated

After your renunciation, you will have the same rights in the US as any other citizen of Canada or whatever country of which you are a citizen.

Note: If you renounce your citizenship:

- You lose the right to live and work in the US.
- You will not be able to vote in US elections.
- You will not be entitled to the protection of the United States when in other parts of the world.
- You will no longer be able to enter and remain indefinitely in the US.
- Any children you have who are born after your renunciation will not receive US citizenship from you (although they may receive US citizenship from the other parent, from birth on US soil, from naturalization later in life, etc.).

Important: There are no temporary renunciations or options to reacquire US citizenship. Renunciation of US citizenship is irrevocable; you lose citizenship for the rest of your life.

After your renunciation, your biometric information — fingerprints and digital photograph — will be taken and stored by the US either when you apply for a visa or when you enter the US. This policy applies to all non-US citizens from the ages of 14 to 79.

3.1 The Reed Amendment

The only law that calls for different treatment of expatriates is the Reed Amendment. In 1996, Congress included a provision in the expatriation law to bar entry to any individual "who officially renounces United States citizenship and who is determined by the Attorney General to have renounced United States citizenship for the purpose of avoiding taxation by the United States."

This amendment added ex-citizens to the list of other "inadmissibles," which includes practicing polygamists, international child abductors, and aliens who have unlawfully voted in US elections.

Note: As of this writing, the Reed Amendment has never been imposed. So, while in theory it is possible that the US could bar you from entry because the Attorney General believes you expatriated with the primary purpose of avoiding US taxation, we think the chances are extremely low that this would ever happen under current law.

4. Tax Planning before You Go

Most of you will not be subject to the expatriation tax, but you should still do some tax planning before giving up your citizenship or green card. The best tax planning opportunities exist only while you are still a US taxpayer and before you become a taxpayer of Canada.

Because a complete discussion of this topic is outside the scope of this book, we will highlight the main issues to consider before leaving the US:

- Should I renounce my US citizenship? What are the pros and cons?
- Should I surrender my green card? What are the pros and cons?
- How should I address the foreign currency issues I will face?
- What should I do with my bank and nonqualified (non-registered) brokerage accounts in the US?
- What should I do with my qualified (registered) accounts (e.g., IRA and 401[k]) in the US?
- I still have registered accounts (e.g., RRSPs) in Canada, should I cash them out before returning to Canada?
- What should I do with my home in the US? If I do not sell it before leaving, what are the tax consequences?
- I have entities such as US corporations or partnerships, what should I do with them?
- If applicable, what should I do about US Social Security and/or Medicare?
- What should I do about health insurance?
- What is the fair market value of all of your capital assets on the date of exit, even if you do not have to file Form 8854, because you will typically want to use these values as your cost basis when you sell those assets in Canada? This could be as easy as statements from your brokerage firm or you may have to go as far as getting appraisals on some of the assets.

4.1 US bank and nonqualified brokerage accounts

When moving to Canada, you will need to decide which accounts you will leave in the US, if any, and what accounts you will close and move to Canada. For bank accounts (checking, savings, certificates of deposit), we recommend that you take most, or all, of the assets to Canada. The problems to be addressed are currency risk and complexity. If you leave your bank accounts in the US you will subject that money to currency exchange risk. However, if you plan on spending time in the US and therefore spending US dollars, you might want to keep some money in the US to spend while visiting.

The second issue to consider is the additional complexity of having a US account. A US account may lead to additional Canadian tax reporting. If you have more than $100,000 CAD in foreign (non-Canadian) assets, you must report them on Form T1135, Foreign Income Verification Statement. If you continue to own a home in the US, you will be over the threshold and you would be required to report the home, the bank accounts, and any other foreign assets.

Note: Canadian banks allow you to have US- and Canadian-dollar dominated accounts, so in most cases there is no real advantage to keeping your bank accounts in the US.

4.2 Nonqualified US brokerage accounts

Determining what to do with your nonqualified brokerage accounts is more complicated than the question of what to do with your bank accounts. Nonqualified brokerage accounts are investment accounts that are not qualified retirement accounts such as a 401(k) or IRA.

The biggest problem is that most financial advisors are not allowed to trade your account once you become a nonresident of the US. This has to do with securities laws and who has jurisdiction/oversight of the advisor trading your account. Only a very small number of advisory firms such as KeatsConnelly are registered in the US and Canada, and can manage your accounts in both countries in a coordinated fashion. Companies such as RBC, TD, and BMO are registered in both countries, but the individual advisors are not, which causes a disconnection in the managing of the accounts.

Canada is an expensive place to invest. In 2012, the Canadian Securities Administrators published a discussion paper[1] and request for comment on Canadian mutual fund fees, which found that Canadian mutual funds are the most expensive in the world. Other problems include:

- Fewer investment choices.

- The Canadian economy is not as diverse as the US's, therefore portfolios are less diverse, which tends to lead to more volatility/risk within the portfolio.

- Required reporting standards are not up to par. While the US has required that investors receive at least quarterly reports and performance results on investment accounts for decades, Canada required reporting for the first time as of July 2016.

- Most advisors in Canada are commissioned salespeople.

---

1   Ontario Securities Commission, "CANADIAN SECURITIES ADMINISTRATORS DISCUSSION PAPER AND REQUEST FOR COMMENT 81-407 MUTUAL FUND FEES," accessed January, 2016. www.osc.gov.on.ca/documents/en/Securities-Category8/csa_2012123_81-407_rfc-mutual-fund-fees.pdf

In summary, if you are a do-it-yourself kind of investor, you will not be able to leave your nonregistered accounts in the US. If you are willing to pay for professional advice you will be limited to a handful of choices, otherwise you will need to close your US accounts and move them to Canada.

4.3 Qualified accounts

With qualified accounts, you will have to leave the accounts in the US or pay the tax to cash them out and move them to Canada. If you cash out your accounts before age 59, you will also be subject to a 10% penalty.

For your qualified accounts, you are forced to find an advisor who will continue to hold your accounts once you become a Canadian resident, or cash your accounts out and pay the tax. In Chapter 6 we go into detail about the possibility of rolling over your IRA to and RRSP. Though it is possible to roll over your IRA to an RRSP, it is typically not a good idea.

4.4 Cashing out your IRA, 401(k), or RRSP

Speaking of possibly cashing out your IRA or 401(k), you can add your RRSP to that consideration if you have one. You will want someone to run the numbers on this, but in some circumstances it may be beneficial to pay tax at the lower US rate today rather than defer the tax and pay a higher rate of tax in Canada.

Ignoring the issues of investing in Canada raised above, the basic question is: Does the deferral outweigh the tax savings? Assuming a 5% return and a 35% tax in the US versus a 50% tax in Canada, it will take 16 years for the deferral to outweigh the lower US tax.

Table 1 shows a year-by-year comparison, assuming the deferred account earns 5% until the year of withdrawal, then it is taxed at 50% in Canada. The other calculation is paying 35% up front and the account grows at an after-tax rate of 3.25% (5% less 35% tax). Another option is to convert your traditional IRA to a Roth before moving to Canada. In this case a 40% tax is paid up front, but no further tax is owing so the Roth grows at 5%. Starting amount is $1,000.

A similar calculation would have to be made when deciding whether it makes sense to convert your traditional IRA to a Roth before moving to Canada. If you convert to a Roth, you will not have to pay the 50% Canadian tax so you would be comparing a higher US tax today, versus allowing the Roth to grow tax-free. You will need to run the calculations based on your actual tax situation, but based on the assumptions above, the Roth conversion is the best choice.

As we explained, we recommend going to a cross-border specialist to get these and other questions answered before you leave the US.

See the Resources at the end of the book for further readings on moving to Canada.

Table 1
COMPARISON WHEN CASHING OUT ACCOUNTS

End of Year	Defer IRA	Defer IRA AfterTax @ 50%	Tax IRA Now @ 35%	Convert to Roth @40%
0	$1,000.00	N/A	$650.00	$600.00
1	$1,050.00	$525.00	$671.13	$630.00
2	$1,102.50	$551.25	$692.94	$661.50
3	$1,157.63	$578.81	$715.46	$694.58
4	$1,215.51	$607.75	$738.71	$729.30
5	$1,276.28	$638.14	$762.72	$765.77
6	$1,340.10	$670.05	$787.51	$804.06
7	$1,407.10	$703.55	$813.10	$844.26
8	$1,477.46	$738.73	$839.53	$886.47
9	$1,551.33	$775.66	$866.81	$930.80
10	$1,628.89	$814.45	$894.98	$977.34
11	$1,710.34	$855.17	$924.07	$1,026.20
12	$1,795.86	$897.93	$954.10	$1,077.51
13	$1,885.65	$942.82	$985.11	$1,131.39
14	$1,979.93	$989.97	$1,017.12	$1,187.96
15	$2,078.93	$1,039.46	$1,050.18	$1,247.36
16	$2,182.87	$1,091.44	$1,084.31	$1,309.72

2

Your First Year in Canada

This chapter looks at things you will need to deal with in your first year in Canada.

1. Overview of Filing Requirements When You Are in Canada

If you are a US citizen or if you retain your green card status after moving to Canada, you will need to prepare tax returns for both countries.

As an American resident in Canada you will need to file Form T1 General with the CRA and a Form 1040 with the IRS. You will generally file one tax return in Canada that includes both federal and provincial taxes, except in Quebec where you will need to file separate federal and provincial returns (Quebec's form is Form TP-1 Quebec and is filed with Revenu Quebec). Though the official language in Quebec is French, all tax forms are also available in English. See Resources at the back of this book for form names and where to find them.

A taxpayer's province or territory of residence is determined by where he or she lived or was a factual resident on December 31 of the tax year. A taxpayer may have moved from one province to another but will file a return based on province or territory of residence on December 31. In that return he or she can allocate income earned in other provinces and pay provincial taxes based on in which province income was earned.

Canadian individual returns are due April 30 unless you or your spouse is self-employed, in which case, the returns are due June 15. Note that the tax owing is due by April 30 even if the return itself is not due until June 15.

You cannot file an extension in Canada. If the return is filed after the due date there may be late penalties even if there is no tax due. Even if you do not have all of the information by the due date of the return, file the return on time and correct it when you get all of the information. In Canada, spouses each need to file their own tax returns, unlike in the United States where spouses can file a "Married Filing Joint" return. Filing separately in Canada is actually beneficial because it avoids the so-called marriage penalty in that each of you get the benefit of the graduated (lower) tax rates. Filing separately also allows for income splitting between spouses or common-law partners.

Even though you and your spouse file your own returns, you need to indicate your marital status since there are certain items that rely on the combined incomes of the spouses. Canada recognizes common-law and same-sex couples if you are living in a conjugal relationship with that person for 12 months; the other person is the parent of your child by birth or adoption; or the other person has custody of your child who is wholly dependent on that person.

In Canada, your world income is subject to Canadian income tax if you are a resident of Canada. If you are not a resident of Canada then you pay tax to Canada only on income earned in Canada.

2. Determining Canadian Residency

We've already covered some of this, but it's all worth repeating. Where a person is "ordinarily resident" is the place where in the settled routine of an individual's life, he or she regularly, normally, or customarily lives. Residence in Canada is based on the relevant facts which include the residential ties in Canada, as well as the purpose and permanence of stays abroad and ties abroad. Significant residential ties to Canada include a home in Canada, a spouse or common-law partner in Canada, and dependents in Canada. Secondary residential ties include the following:

- personal property in Canada (i.e., automobile or furniture);
- economic ties to Canada such that your income is mostly from Canada;
- social ties to Canada such as memberships in clubs or religious organizations;
- driver's license issued by a Canadian province or territory;
- citizenship; and
- health insurance issued by a Canadian province or territory.

If you have not established residential ties to Canada but have spent more than 183 days in Canada during the calendar year, you would be considered a resident of Canada for tax purposes and pay tax on your world income from the first day you are a deemed resident of Canada.

The Convention between Canada and the United States of America with Respect to Taxes on Income and Capital, better known as the Canada-US Tax Treaty, or simply the Treaty, includes factors similar to those indicated above for determining in which country a taxpayer is resident. It also has a mechanism for resolving the residency issues by "competent authority," which is a tribunal of Canadian and US officials that will resolve the issue if all else fails.

3. First Things First

When arriving in Canada during the year, you will need to file a part-year resident return. On the T1 General return you will indicate your arrival date in Canada and will be responsible for reporting income from the date you entered through December 31, and pay tax on your world income, as well as any income earned from Canadian sources prior to establishing residency in Canada.

You will need a Social Insurance Number (SIN) in order to file a T1 return. You will also need a SIN for government benefits, to arrange for certain banking services, and to work for an employer in Canada. You will need to apply for one in person at a Service Canada office. The SIN is a nine-digit number and is issued in paper format.

Social Insurance Numbers are issued with the first digit "9" to temporary workers who are neither Canadian citizens nor residents; these are issued with an expiry date coinciding with the work authorization document allowing them to work in Canada. When the immigration status changes to that of a landed immigrant you will need to apply for a new SIN and the new number will not begin with a "9." After you have obtained the new SIN, do not use the old number.

4. Deemed Acquisitions

If you owned certain properties, other than taxable Canadian properties, while you were a nonresident of Canada, you are considered to have disposed of the properties and to have immediately reacquired them at a cost equal to their fair market value on the date you became a resident of Canada. This is called a deemed acquisition.

Usually, the fair market value is the highest dollar value you can get for your property in a normal business transaction. You should keep a record of the fair market value of your properties on the date you arrived in

Canada. The fair market value will be your cost when you calculate your gain or loss from selling the property in the future.

5. First-Year Tax Filing

When moving from the US to Canada, you will likely also have to file a final US state income tax return that indicates you moved out of the state sometime during the year and were therefore a part-year resident.

Other Canadian forms may need to be filed that deal with foreign reporting issues. Keep in mind that there are large penalties for late filing or non-filing of these forms. The forms and circumstances for reporting foreign issues are highly dependent on your personal circumstances and are not appropriate for us to go into detail on here. Be sure to advise whomever prepares your Canadian return that such circumstances exist, if applicable.

However, one form that is very common is Form T1135, Foreign Income Verification Statement (similar in nature to the US Foreign Bank Account Reporting), and you need to file this report if you have specified foreign property costing more than $100,000 CAD at any time in the year. Specified property includes —

- funds or intangible property (i.e., patents or copyrights) held outside Canada;
- tangible property held outside Canada;
- a share of the capital stock of a nonresident corporation;
- shares of Canadian resident corporations held outside Canada (i.e., through a foreign broker);
- debt owed by a nonresident including government or corporate bonds, debentures, mortgages, and notes receivable;
- an interest in a foreign insurance policy;
- precious metals and futures contracts held outside Canada;
- an interest in a nonresident trust;
- an interest in a foreign partnership that holds specified foreign property unless the partnership is required to file a T1135; and
- property that is convertible or rights to acquire property that is specified foreign property.

Specified property does not include —

- property exclusively used or held in carrying on a business;
- a share of the capital stock of a foreign affiliate;
- an interest in certain trusts designated as exempt trusts;

- a personal use property such as a vacation property; and
- an interest or right to acquire any of the above excluded foreign properties.

Form T1135 must be filed by the due date of the tax return that is either April 30 or June 15. Penalties for late filing of this, and other forms, are $25 per day with a minimum penalty of $100 and a maximum penalty of $2,500. Penalties for late filing of your T1 return, as mentioned in Chapter 1, are 5% of the balance owing plus 1% per month of your balance owing for each full month your return is late to a maximum of 12 months. If you have been charged a late filing penalty in a prior year, the late filing penalties are doubled to 10% of balance owing plus 2% for each late month.

In the year you first become resident you do not have to file these forms but the exemption is only for the first year of residency. If you are a returning resident to Canada you still need to file these forms even in the year you become resident in Canada.

When you arrive in Canada, you will be deemed to have acquired your assets at the fair market value of the property when you became resident in Canada. That will become your adjusted cost base to calculate your capital gain in Canada upon disposition of the asset. As an example, if you owned a share of Apple stock that you purchased for $25, and when you became a resident of Canada the stock traded at $120, and then you sold the stock when you were a resident of Canada for $130, you would only have a gain in Canada of $10 and pay tax in Canada on the gain of $10. Note that as a US citizen you would report the gain on your US tax return as $105 and pay tax in the US on that gain, and you would receive a foreign tax credit for the tax paid to Canada.

As a further example of this, if a taxpayer owned real estate in the US prior to becoming a resident of Canada, then for Canadian purposes the adjusted cost base of that real estate would be the fair market value of the real estate on the date the taxpayer immigrated to Canada. This is because you are taxed in Canada on your world income only while you are a resident of Canada and if there was any gain on the property prior to immigrating to Canada that gain would not be taxed in Canada; the full amount of the gain would be taxed in the US.

Note: There is no form to file or election to make to have the basis of your assets stepped up. You must keep a record of the fair market values on the date you become a resident, along with supporting evidence of those values. When selling the assets in the future you will use those values as the purchase price.

Unfortunately, the expenses of moving to Canada are not deductible on your Canadian return for Canadian tax purposes, although the expenses will generally be deductible on your US return if moving for work. If you can get your employer to reimburse your expenses, your moving expenses will not be taxable provided that the reimbursed expenses are reasonable and necessary for the move.

When you move from the US to Canada you may end up renting your home in the US. The rental income and expenses would have to be reported in Canada and tax would be payable on the net rental income. If a loss is incurred you may be able to deduct the loss in Canada against other income, provided there is an expectation of profit. In Canada, capital cost allowance (Canada's version of depreciation) cannot be claimed if it increases or creates a loss, whereas depreciation is always taken in the US, so the net rental income for Canadian tax purposes will be different than the net rental income for US purposes.

Note: Though taking capital cost allowance is not required, we recommend that it be taken whenever possible to keep the difference between US and Canadian gains or losses as small as possible. For the foreign tax credit to work most efficiently, the income (or loss) should be as close as possible. See Chapter 5 for details of the foreign tax credit.

6. Contributions to Retirement Plans

There is no deduction in Canada for US retirement plan contributions to either a traditional Individual Retirement Account (IRA) or Roth IRA. In certain circumstances, contributions to a US employer-sponsored plan, such as a 401(k), are deductible in Canada and can be deducted in a similar manner to a Canadian registered retirement plan. A taxpayer may make contributions to a Canadian retirement plan such as a Registered Retirement Savings Plan (RRSP), based on his or her prior year's earned income. Earned income in Canada is basically salary or wages, net self-employed business income, net rental income, disability pension, and taxable alimony income.

Note: The definition of earned income is different in Canada and the US The big difference is that while Canada treats net rental income as earned income, the US does not. The RRSP contribution limit is the lesser of 18% of your prior year's earned income and $25,370 (in 2016). This is known as RRSP contribution room. In the first year you arrive in Canada you will not have a prior year's earned income (from a Canadian perspective) and therefore cannot make an RRSP contribution. If you are a returning resident to Canada, you may have RRSP room and may make a deductible contribution in your first year back in Canada. Contributions to RRSPs can be made during the year and up to 60 days after year-end. After your Canadian return is filed, Canada Revenue Agency (CRA) will provide you with your Notice of Assessment, which outlines how the return was assessed and will include your RRSP contribution room for the next tax year.

6.1 RRSP deduction limit formula

Here is a formula for determining RRSP deduction limits.

RRSP deduction limit = A + B + R - C, where

A is your unused RRSP deduction room at the end of the preceding tax year.

B is the amount, if any, by which

    (a) the lesser of the RRSP dollar limit for the year and 18% of your earned income for the preceding tax year, exceeds the total of all amounts

    (b) your pension adjustment for the preceding tax year in respect of an employer, or

    (c) a prescribed amount in respect of the taxpayer for the year,

C is your net past service pension adjustment for the year, and

R is your total pension adjustment reversal for the year.

Note: One very big difference in Canada is when you do not contribute the maximum allowable RRSP contribution, the difference will carry forward to future years.

For those immigrants to Canada who have a Roth IRA when they arrive in Canada, an election must be filed with your first Canadian tax return. The election identifies the Roth IRA and the balance in the Roth IRA when the taxpayer immigrated to Canada. As long as there are no further contributions to the Roth IRA while a resident of Canada there will be no tax in Canada on the income earned in the Roth IRA, or on distributions from the Roth IRA, while resident in Canada. Basically, Canada will allow the Roth IRA to remain tax free; however, this treatment will not be allowed on any new investments to a Roth IRA after you have become a resident of Canada.

Important: If you make contributions to a Roth IRA after you are a resident of Canada, you will lose your deferral and the income from interest, dividends, and capital gains must be reported on your Canadian return.

The Treaty allows for the continued deferral of your traditional IRA and therefore no election is needed for your IRA to be tax-deferred in Canada.

Withdrawals from traditional IRAs are taxable in Canada, the same as they are in the US. Any tax paid on the withdrawal in the US will be allowable as a foreign tax credit in Canada.

7. Social Security

Under the Treaty, the country of residence has the exclusive right to tax social security benefits. Therefore as an American resident in Canada, you will report US Social Security income only on your Canadian tax return and not on your US return. However, you must file Form 8833 — Treaty-Based Return Position Disclosure to report to the IRS that you received Social Security benefits, but are not reporting the income, per the Treaty. Canada permits a deduction of 15% of the Social Security benefit, so the taxpayer ends up paying tax in Canada on only 85% of the Social Security benefit. Canadian residents who have been receiving US Social Security since before 1996 receive an additional 35% reduction (50% tax free).

Americans who are also recipients of Canada Pension/Quebec Pension and/or Old Age Security, and are residents of Canada, need not include these amounts on their US returns as they are treated as Social Security under the Treaty. However, the benefits must be reported on Form 8833.

8. Differences in How Certain Income Is Taxed

8.1 Dividends

Dividends received from Canadian corporations are reported on a gross-up basis and subject to a dividend tax credit so that they are taxed in Canada at a preferred rate, whereas in the US they are reported on an actual received basis. The reason for the gross-up in Canada is because Canada has a system of integration whereby the tax would be the same as if the taxpayer received the income directly, as compared to it being received in a corporation and the net income after tax is distributed to the shareholders. In theory, the total tax paid by the individual if the income is received directly would be the same as if the income were received by a corporation; the corporate tax paid on the income would result in a net distribution to the shareholder and the shareholder would pay tax on the dividend received. This does not work out perfectly because it depends on the provincial tax rates, so that in some provinces there is "over-integration" and some provinces "under-integration." However under the most recent tax rules in Canada the system of integration is as near perfect as it has ever been. US citizen taxpayers resident in Canada will need to report their dividend income from Canadian corporations on a grossed up basis on their Canadian returns and on an actual received amount on their US returns. Most public company dividends that are from non-US domestic corporations are treated as "qualified dividends" and are taxed in the US at preferred tax rates. Any dividend income received from non-Canadian corporations is reported in the Canadian return at actual amounts and is taxed at ordinary rates in Canada.

8.2 Capital gains

While Canada taxes 50% of a capital gain at the marginal rate, the US will tax the entire gain of assets held more than a year at a lower, preferred rate ranging from 0–20%. Based on the highest marginal rates in Canada, the effective tax rates for capital gains vary from approximately 20–26%. In the US, short-term gains (those held one year or less) are taxed at your marginal rate which would be up to 39.6% at the top marginal federal rate. In addition, capital gains (long- or short-term) could be subject to an additional 3.8% Net Investment Income Tax.

Note: In Canada there is no distinction between short- or long-term gains.

8.3 Gambling winnings

Gambling winnings are taxable in the US whereas they are not taxable in Canada. Under the Treaty, residents of Canada can deduct their US gambling losses against their US gambling winnings if they elect to file a US tax return. You must also file Form 8833.

8.4 Registered accounts

In Canada income earned in an RRSP is deferred until there is a distribution. Under the Canada-US Tax treaty, income earned in an RRSP can be deferred in the US until such time that there is a distribution from the RRSP, which aids in avoiding any foreign tax credit mismatch because the income becomes taxable in the US at the same time it becomes taxable in Canada. With regard to the distributions of the RRSP, the entire amount is taxable in Canada since there was a deduction allowed in Canada when there was a contribution to an RRSP. However, for Americans resident in Canada who contributed to an RRSP, there was no deduction for the contribution on their US returns. Therefore the amount contributed to the RRSP by the US citizen is considered basis in the US so that the total amount of the distribution would not be taxable in the US.

Note: States are not required to follow the terms of the Treaty, however most do. California does not allow for the deferral of the earnings within a Canadian registered account; you must report and pay tax to California on income that occurs within your RRSP, LIRA, RRIF, etc.

8.5 Alimony

As an American (US citizen or green card holder), alimony received is taxable and alimony paid is deductible.

Caution: Be careful not to confuse the rules for Americans with the rules for nonresidents of the US. As a nonresident of the US (which you are not if you are a US citizen or green card holder), alimony is only taxable in the country of residence. From a tax perspective, an American living in Canada is not a nonresident of the US.

9. Deductions and Credits

In Canada, you can claim personal amounts as nonrefundable credits against your taxes payable. These personal amounts consist of a basic amount, $11,474 in 2016 and a spousal amount of the same amount which is reduced dollar for dollar by the spouse's net income. There is also an age amount of $7,125 for taxpayers over 65 and it is eliminated on income greater than $83,427 in 2016.

There are also eligible dependent credits as well as infirm tax credits. When you become a resident of Canada these personal tax credits are prorated by the number of days in the year you were resident in Canada. There is an exception to this rule if your income in the year of immigration is greater than 90% of your total income. In that case, you can claim 100% of the personal amounts. Some personal credit amounts are never restricted by your length of residence. Those credits are: charitable donations, tuition fees, disability amount for self, Canada or Quebec pension plan contributions, Canadian Employment Insurance premiums, and interest paid in the year on loans for postsecondary education.

Tuition fees are deductible by the student for attending a qualifying postsecondary institution inside or outside Canada. The student is entitled to a deduction of the tuition fees plus, for a full-time student, $400 per month that he or she was a full-time student as well as a textbook credit of $65 per month for that time. Part-time students can receive a deduction of $120 per month as well as a textbook credit of $20 per month that they were part-time students. The sum of these amounts becomes a tax credit of 15% of the amount (e.g., a $400 deduction converts to a $60 credit). Any amounts not used by the student can be carried forward indefinitely to a future year when the student has enough income to use these credits. In addition, up to $5,000 of these credits can be transferred per year to a parent or grandparent to use on a Canadian tax return.

There are additional credits of up to $1,000 per year for enrolling a child in a fitness or sports program or up to $1,000 for enrolling a child in an arts program, as well as credits for enrollment in artistic, cultural, recreational, or development activities.

Canada provides a First-Time Home Buyers' Tax Credit that is worth 15% of $5,000 of qualifying expenditures, or $750. A qualifying expenditure would be the cost of a new home or costs associated with purchasing a new home in Canada. The credit can be claimed by either spouse or split between each spouse. To be eligible for this credit neither the individual nor the individual's spouse or common-law partner can have owned and lived in another home anywhere in Canada in the year of the home purchase or four preceding calendar years.

Medical expenses paid while you are resident in Canada would be eligible for a tax credit. You can claim medical expenses for any 12-month period but you cannot claim any medical expenses already claimed in a prior year. Medical expenses will be reduced by 3% of your net income and a 15% non-refundable credit can be used against tax payable. As an example, if you have $2,000 of medical expenses incurred while resident in Canada and your income is $20,000, then your medical expenses available for credit would be $2,000 less $600 ($20,000 x 3%) or $1,400. In addition, if you meet the 90% income in Canada rule mentioned above, you can claim all of your medical expenses for the year.

Note: Deductions in Canada are converted to credits using the lowest marginal tax rate of 15%. Therefore $100 of deductible expense is converted to a $15 credit and is worth $15 to you. In the US, the worth of a deduction depends on your marginal tax bracket. If you are in the 25% tax bracket, a $100 deduction would be worth $25 to you.

10. US Filing Requirements

US citizens and those who continue to hold green cards are required to file US returns and report their worldwide income. Residents of Canada also have to file a Canadian tax return and report their worldwide income.

Relief exists so that US citizens who are also Canadian residents do not end up paying tax on the same income to both Canada and the US. This is provided by the Treaty through the mechanism of foreign tax credits. In Canada you may be able to claim this credit if you paid foreign taxes on income received outside of Canada and reported on the Canadian return. This credit reduces the amount of tax payable on your Canadian return since you have paid the foreign tax to the foreign tax authority on the foreign income. In the US, the foreign tax credit also is intended to reduce the double-tax burden that would otherwise arise when foreign source income is taxed by both the US and the foreign country from which the income is derived.

In order to qualify, the tax must be an actual foreign tax liability that is imposed. That tax must be paid or accrued and must be an income tax as opposed to taxes such as a VAT or property tax. The foreign tax credit in the US is not a dollar-for-dollar credit. It is based on the percentage of foreign income to total income reported on the US return. In theory, if all the income reported on the US return was foreign then you would get a foreign tax credit of all foreign taxes paid. Any unused foreign tax credits can be carried back 1 year and forward 10 years. This means that you have up to 12 years to use foreign taxes paid as a foreign tax credit; current year, previous year, and 10 years into the future.

There also exists another mechanism in the US Internal Revenue Code to alleviate double tax. If you are a US citizen or a resident alien of the US and you live outside of the US, you are taxed on your worldwide income. However, you can qualify to exclude from your income an amount of your foreign earnings. In 2016 this amount was up to $101,300. In order to qualify for this inclusion, your tax home must be in a foreign country or must be physically present in a foreign country for 330 days during any period of 12 consecutive months.

11. The Totalization Agreement

Canada and the US have entered into a treaty of sorts on Social Security known as the Canada — United States Social Security Agreement (a.k.a., Totalization Agreement).

The agreement became effective August 1, 1984. The intent of the agreement is to improve Social Security protection for people who work or have worked in both countries. It also helps protect the benefit rights of people who have earned Canadian Social Security credits based on residence and/or contributions in Canada.

Because the Canadian Social Security system includes a special pension plan operated in the Province of Quebec, an additional understanding has been concluded with Quebec to extend the agreement to that province. This also became effective August 1, 1984. Terms of the US-Canada agreement and US-Quebec understanding are very similar, and except where otherwise noted, references in this document to the US-Canada agreement also apply to the US-Quebec understanding.

The agreement with Canada helps many people who would otherwise not be eligible for monthly retirement, disability or survivor's benefits under the Social Security systems of one or both countries. It also helps people who would otherwise have to pay Social Security taxes to both countries on the same earnings. For example, you can qualify for and receive US Social Security with as few as 6 credits of coverage when you combine the credits earned in Canada. Without the Totalization Agreement, you would have to work at least ten years in the US to qualify for Social Security.

For the United States, the agreement covers Social Security taxes (including the US Medicare portion) and Social Security retirement, disability and survivor's insurance benefits, however it does not cover benefits under the US Medicare program or the Supplemental Security Income program. For Canada, the agreement applies to the Old Age Security program and the Canada Pension Plan. The understanding with Quebec applies to the Quebec Pension Plan.

12. Canadian Health Insurance

All Canadian citizens and permanent residents are entitled to apply for public health insurance. When you have it, you do not pay for most healthcare services as healthcare is paid for through taxes. When you use public healthcare services, you must show your health insurance card to the hospital or medical clinic.

All provinces and territories will provide free emergency medical services, even if you do not have a government health card. If you have an emergency, go to the nearest hospital. If you go to a walk-in clinic in a province or territory where you are not a resident, you might be charged a fee.

Each province and territory has its own health insurance plan. Make sure you know what your plan covers. Government health insurance plans give you access to basic medical services. You may also need private insurance to pay for things that government plans do not fully cover. The most common types of plans are extended health plans. These cover costs for items such as:

- prescription medications
- dental care
- physiotherapy
- ambulance services
- prescription eyeglasses

If you work, check with your employer to see if extra coverage is offered through it.

New residents in some provinces must wait a certain period (up to three months) before receiving government health insurance (contact your provincial or territorial Ministry of Health to know how long you will need to wait, but at the time of writing, only Alberta, New Brunswick, Nova Scotia, and Prince Edward Island had no waiting period). Make sure you have private health insurance to cover your healthcare needs during this waiting period.

See the Resources at the back of this book for links to provincial healthcare websites.

3

An Overview of Canadian Taxation

In this chapter, we will discuss not only the basics of Canadian tax, but compare and contrast the US and Canadian tax systems, including a brief history and background of each.

The Canadian *Income Tax Act* (the "Act" or "ITA") is the Canadian equivalent of the US Internal Revenue Code (the "Code" or "IRC"). This book will cover a very small segment of the Act, and even for the sections of the Act we do discuss, we will limit our discussion to the basics.

1. Two Important Points to Set the Stage

There are two basic points we want to make sure are clear and said up front; while the US imposes a tax on its residents and citizens, Canada's tax system is based on residency only, not citizenship. In fact, the US and Eritrea (a small African country north of Ethiopia and east of Sudan) are the only two countries that base their systems of taxation on both residence and citizenship. Other countries tax the worldwide income of residents, but do not tax their own citizens living elsewhere. So on the one hand, if you are a citizen of the US you are taxed on your world income no matter where you live and no matter where the income is generated. On the other hand, if you are a citizen of Canada and leave Canada, you are no longer taxed on your world income by Canada, you are only taxed on your Canadian income.

The other point is that with the tax increase that resulted from the 2015 budget, the spread between Canadian and US taxes is near or at its greatest.

The Canadian tax burden can be 50% more than what it would be in the US. Comparing marginal tax rates is misleading because what matters is the amount of tax paid. In addition to marginal tax rates being generally lower in the US, the main reasons the US tax is lower than Canada is due to three factors:

- **Wider marginal tax brackets:** Expressed in Canadian dollars, the top federal marginal tax bracket does not begin until you have taxable income of approximately $648,500 CAD ($466,950.72 USD = $648,541 CAD at time of writing), whereas you are in the top Canadian federal marginal tax bracket at only $200,000 CAD of taxable income. That means you are paying the highest marginal tax in Canada on approximately $450,000 CAD that you wouldn't in the US.

- **Difference in gross and taxable income:** There are very few ways to shelter income in Canada. The two primary ways to shelter income are contributing to your RRSP and accumulating income in a Canadian corporation. In the US there are a number of expenses that can be deducted against your gross income that are not allowed in Canada, such as state, local income taxes, property taxes, and principal mortgage interest. In addition, there are tax-free and tax-deferred savings vehicles such as municipal bonds, annuities, tax-deferred exchange of like-kind assets, etc. So if you have $100,000 of gross income in Canada, you might end up with $85,000 or more of taxable income. In the US, you would most likely end up with taxable income of around $70,000.

- **Canadian deductions converted to credits using the lowest marginal rate:** In the US, a deduction is worth the amount of the expense times the marginal tax rate. In Canada, your deduction is converted to a tax credit using the lowest marginal tax rate (15%). This means that in Canada you get back $0.15 on every dollar of deductible expense, whereas if you were in the 33% marginal tax bracket in the US, you would get back $0.33 on every deductible expense.

In addition to income tax, Canada also imposes property taxes, Goods and Services Tax (a.k.a., sales tax), and transfer taxes, to name the most common taxes an individual is likely to pay. Since property taxes in Canada are similar to those in the US, we will not elaborate further here.

Goods and Services Tax (GST) is one of three different ways sales tax is collected in Canada. GST is a 5% federal sales tax. Provinces also impose a Provincial Sales Tax (PST) varying from 0–10%. Quebec has its own version of the PST called the Quebec Sales Tax or QST. Its rate is 9.975%. Ontario, New Brunswick, Newfoundland and Labrador, Nova Scotia, and Prince Edward Island have a Harmonized Sales Tax (HST), which is a combination of GST and PST into one tax that the federal government administers.

2. History of Canada Revenue Agency (CRA)

Prior to 1917, the Canadian government did not have an income tax, but when World War I came along, the cost of the war forced Canada to adopt an income tax so that the war effort could be financed.

The constitutional authority for the federal income tax is found in section 91 paragraph 3 of the *Constitution Act*, 1867, which assigns to the federal Parliament power over "the raising of money by any mode or system of taxation." The constitutional authority for the various provincial income taxes is found in section 92 paragraph 2 of the *Constitution Act*, which assigns to the legislature of each province the power of "Direct Taxation within the Province in order to the raising of a Revenue for Provincial Purposes."

For many years the agency responsible for collecting taxes was referred to as Revenue Canada, and then in 1999 the government reorganized the agency's responsibilities to include customs enforcement. However, just four years later in 2003, customs enforcement was removed and the agency again changed its name, this time to Canada Revenue Agency (CRA). To this day, many people still refer to the agency as Revenue Canada. Don't be confused; Canada Revenue Agency, CRA, and Revenue Canada all refer to the same thing.

The Mission of the CRA is "to administer tax, benefits, and related programs, and to ensure compliance on behalf of government across Canada, thereby contributing to the ongoing economic and social well-being of Canadians."

The Minister of National Revenue is a politician responsible for overseeing the CRA and reporting to parliament. The minister delegates the duties to the Commissioner of Revenue and Chief Executive Officer of the CRA, a government employee. The Commissioner is also the head of the Board of Management that oversees the CRA. The Board is made up of 15 members, 11 of which are nominated by the provinces and territories. Whereas the Minister of National Revenue is a member of the majority party in power and his or her term can be long or short depending on whether he or she is re-elected and the party remains in control, in the US the IRS's Commissioner of Internal Revenue is appointed by the President of the United States and serves a five-year term.

The CRA has its head office in Ottawa and is further divided into five regions, each of which has a few Tax Services offices which perform audits and collections. There are also seven Taxation Centers that process and review tax returns that have been filed.

Note: Tax Services offices are different than the Taxation Centers that you will typically be dealing with. These two offices may or may not be in the same building. Be sure that you have the correct address for your purpose before mailing or visiting an office.

3. Filing Requirements in Canada

As a resident of Canada, you are taxed based on worldwide income and a tax is imposed at the federal and provincial level. The exception: In Quebec, the federal government collects the tax on behalf of the provinces and territories, and distributes the money to them upon collection. If you are living in Quebec, you will need to file separate federal and Quebec returns, the same way you file separate federal and state return in the US. Returns are available in French or English in all provinces.

For the year you arrive in Canada, you must report your world income from the date you became a resident through December 31. As an American (US citizen or green card holder), you will also have to file a US return reporting your worldwide income for the entire year, just as you always have. This means that the income earned while a resident of Canada will be reported to the US and Canada. To avoid double tax, you will need to use the foreign tax credit, which is discussed in great detail in Chapter 5.

One thing to note that is different: if filing a paper version of your Canadian return, you must attach all of your receipts to your return. If filing electronically, you will not attach the receipts, but you must keep all of the receipts in case CRA asks for them.

You will have to file a return in Canada if any of the following situations apply:

- You owe tax (i.e., withholding was not sufficient).
- You want to claim a refund (i.e., withholding was too much).
- CRA requested that you file a return.
- You received working income tax benefit advance payments.
- You or your spouse or common-law partner elected to split pension income.
- You disposed of capital property (real estate or securities) or you were attributed a taxable capital gain (from a mutual fund, for example).
- You have to repay any of your Old Age Security (OAS) or Employment Insurance (EI) benefits.
- You have not repaid all amounts withdrawn from your registered retirement savings plan, under the Home Buyers' Plan or Lifelong Learning Plan.
- You have contributed to the Canada Pension Plan.

- You are paying Employment Insurance premiums on self-employment or other eligible earnings.
- You want to claim a credit of any sort.
- You have incurred a non-capital loss that you want to be able to apply in other years (a carryforward).
- You want to carry forward or transfer the unused part of your tuition, education, and textbook amounts.
- You want to report income for which you could contribute to an RRSP and/or a pooled registered pension plan.
- You want to carry forward any unused investment tax credit on expenditures you incurred during the current year.
- You receive the guaranteed income supplement or allowance benefits under the Old Age Security program.

Important: The tax filing deadline in Canada is April 30 of each year (June 15 for self-employed Canadian businesses) and no extension of time to file is allowed. If April 30 falls on a weekend, the return is due on the first working day following it. You will want to file your US return first and take the tax paid in the US as a credit against your Canadian tax. Therefore, it is important to have your US return prepared no later than early April, if at all possible. If you cannot have your US return prepared in time, you will have to file your Canadian return without all of the information, and then when your US return is complete, you can file an adjusted Canadian return. If you must file an adjusted return, be sure to wait for your Notice of Assessment from CRA before filing the adjustment. You will need to make your adjustments on Form T1 — Adjustment Request.

Note: See Chapter 2: Your First Year in Canada for more information about filing your first Canadian return.

The Notice of Assessment is the form that Canada Revenue Agency sends to all taxpayers after processing their returns. It states the amount of taxes to be paid or refunded. If Canada Revenue Agency has made any corrections to your income tax form, the Notice of Assessment explains what changes have been made. If you disagree with the Notice of Assessment you have received, the first thing to do is to contact Canada Revenue Agency. If you still disagree after discussing the matter with the CRA, you can make a formal objection, as long as you do it within 90 days of the date on the Notice of Assessment.

3.1 Unwinding a previous deemed disposition

If you are returning to Canada after having left October 1, 1996 or later, you can make an election to adjust the deemed disposition you reported when you exited Canada. This is known as unwinding your deemed disposition.

You can only make this election if you still own property that was deemed to be disposed of when you exited earlier. If you make this election on "taxable Canadian property," you can reduce the gain reported on the return in the year you exited Canada.

You make this election by sending the International and Ottawa Tax Services Office your request by the filing due date, generally April 30 of the year following the year of you becoming a resident. You must include a list of the properties you own and the fair market value of each property for which you are making the election.

4. Summary of Major Differences between Canadian and US Taxes

Although we will go into more detail in later chapters, some of the major differences between US and Canadian tax are:

- Canadian tax is based on residency; once you are no longer a resident, you are generally not subject to Canadian tax. Only Eritrea and the United States tax their citizens on their worldwide income, regardless of where they live in the world.

- Tax filing deadline is April 30 in Canada (June 15 if self-employed).

- There is no extension of time to file in Canada; although if you have taxes owing, you can file and at a later time file a corrected return.

- Married individuals file separately (this is may be an opportunity for tax planning).

- All tax slips, regardless of whether tax was withheld or not, must be attached to the return. Proof (receipts) of deductions must be attached to the return, unless filing electronically. However, returns are generally required to be filed electronically.

- There is no deduction for taxes paid, of any kind.

- There is no deduction for principal home mortgage interest.

- With few exceptions such as retirement plans, there is no deferral of income. Examples of deferrals that are not allowed are annuities, and "like-kind" exchanges of real estate.

- There is no such thing as tax-free income, such as from municipal bonds.

Each year, after filing your return, you will receive a notice of assessment notifying you that you do, or do not, owe any additional tax, as well as your RRSP contribution limit and amount of carryovers, if any (discussed later). **The Notice of Assessment is as important as your tax return and you should treat it as such by keeping it in a safe place along with your tax returns.**

5. Filing Requirements in the US

All US citizens and non-citizens that are residents (resident aliens) are required to file a US tax return if they meet certain income thresholds. To be clear, if you are considered a resident of the US, you are subject to the tax laws of the US, even if you are there illegally. You are a resident alien if you meet one of the following tests —

1. You are a legal permanent resident, e.g., green card holder, or

2. You meet a 183-day substantial presence test. This is a two-part test and if you fail the first part of the test, you are generally a US resident, with limited exceptions. If you fail only the second part of the test, you can file Form 8840 to claim a closer connection to a foreign country (Canada) and will not be considered a US resident, assuming that you do have a closer connection to Canada.

Part one of the substantial presence test: You are physically present in the US at least 183 days during the calendar year. Note that each partial day counts as one full day. The only exception is if you are flying and you simply pass through the US on your way to another foreign destination.

Part two of the test: You are physically present in the US for at least 183 days using the three-year formula below. Current year is X.

Year X: each day counts as one day

Year X-1: each three days count as one day

Year X-2: each six days count as one day

For example, if you spent 122 days in the US each year, each of the last three years, this is what you would have:

In 2016, you spent 122 days, times 1/1 =   122 days

In 2015, you spent 122 days, times 1/3 =   41 days

In 2014, you spent 122 days, times 1/6 =   20 days

Total number of days using the formula, equals 183 days so you fail Part 2 of the test and are considered a US resident, unless you file IRS Form 8840 showing that you have closer connections to Canada.

Many Americans living in Canada have Canadian spouses who are not US residents or green card holders; see more about the substantial presence test in Chapter 11, section 4.

Note: If you arrive in the US on November 1 and leave on March 31, you would have been in the US a total of 121 days. If you did this year in and year out, you would pass the second part of the test most years. Every leap year, you would have stayed in the US 122 days and therefore failed the test and would need to file IRS Form 8840 to avoid being considered a US resident and being subject to tax.

What makes this rule confusing is the fact that the test has two parts and immigration has different rules. Being in the US for less than 183 days is only one part of the test. If you are in the US every year for 122 days or more, you have failed part two of the test and must file Form 8840 to show the IRS that you are not a US resident because you have closer connections to Canada. If you fail the second part of the test and do not file Form 8840, you are a US taxpayer and subject to US tax. An estimated 1 million Canadians in the US are residents and not filing returns. It is this group of Canadians — those that spend four months or more each year in the US and not filing Form 8840 — to which we are mostly referring.

With regards to immigration rules, and dealing with border agents, the easiest way to explain the difference is to say they are looking at a rolling 12-month period versus the calendar year the IRS uses. For example, if you stay in the US from October 1 through April 1, you would have been in the US 183 consecutive days, yet you would only be in the US for 92 days in the first year and 91 days in the second year. If you assume no other days in the US in either year, you clearly passed both parts of the residency test for tax purposes, but failed the test for immigration purposes. To make matters worse, the customs agents are not consistent in their application of the rules.

If you are a resident or citizen, you still may not have to file a tax return if your income is below certain thresholds. Table 2 shows the income thresholds for two categories.

There are other categories and corresponding thresholds. If these categories do not apply to you, please check the instructions to determine if you are required to file.

Table 2
DO YOU HAVE TO FILE A US 2015 FEDERAL TAX RETURN?

If you are considered a US resident and you are:	You must file if gross income is at least:
Single	
Under age 65	$10,150
Age 65 or older	$11,700
Married, filing jointly, and living together	
Both spouses under age 65	$20,300
One spouse under age 65	$21,500
Both spouses age 65 or older	$22,700

Note: The US defines marriage as a man and a woman who are legally married. If you are in a common-law or same-sex relationship, you cannot file as married for federal tax purposes. Some states allow for these types of relationships, but that does not change how you file your federal return.

When filing Forms 1040 or 1040NR, double check the IRS' mailing address as it does change from time to time and can be different depending on whether you are enclosing payment.

5.1 When to file your individual income tax return

The normal due date for filing individual income tax returns (Form 1040) is April 15 of the year following the tax year. If this date falls on a weekend, the due date is the Monday following the weekend. You can get an automatic six-month extension of time to file your return by filing Form 4868 by the due date, typically April 15. By filing this form in a timely fashion, your time to file will be extended to October 15.

Caution: An extension provides only an extension of time to file, not to pay your taxes. You must calculate and pay any taxes due by April 15 (or the adjusted date) to avoid penalties. If you are required to make estimated (installment) tax payments, you must make those payments even though your return is on extension. Not all forms that you may need to file have the same due date. Those forms will also have their own forms to file for an extension for that form, and that form only. Not only do some forms have different due dates, some do not allow for an extension of time to file. For example, Form 3520-A for reporting foreign trusts is due on March 15 and Form 7004 is required for the six-month extension, which means that the ultimate filing deadline is September 15, not October 15 like most of the rest of your return. Beginning in 2016, FinCEN Form 114 is due April 15, but a six month extension will be available.

Also, filing an extension does not increase your chance of being audited. If fact, if you cannot get your tax information to the accountant early in the season, you may want the accountant to file an extension so that the accountant can prepare the return after April 15 when there is less pressure and they haven't been working 12–16-hour days for the previous two months.

5.2 Electronic filing

Paid preparers are now required to file all tax returns electronically, when possible. However, some returns have forms or situations that have not yet been approved for electronic filing. When electronically filing, our accountant will require you to sign Form 8453, U.S. Individual Income Tax Transmittal for IRS *e-file* Return.

6. Penalties and Interest for Underpayments, Late Filings, and Late Payments

6.1 United States

If it is determined later (by you or the IRS) that the amount of tax owed is greater than the tax paid when the return was filed, there will be interest due on the underpayment of tax. The interest rate can change quarterly, but is currently 3% for underpayments. The interest is compounded daily.

If you file your return late without a reasonable cause the IRS will impose a penalty of 5% per month, with a maximum penalty of 25%. If your return is more than 60 days late, the IRS imposes a minimum penalty equal to the lesser of $135 or 100% of the tax due. If the failure to file is fraudulent, the monthly penalty is 15%, with a maximum penalty of 75%.

If you are late in paying your taxes, the penalty is 0.5% per month, with a maximum penalty of 25%. This penalty is in addition to the regular interest charge. This penalty may be doubled (to 1%) if after repeated requests to pay and a notice of levy, you do not pay.

As mentioned earlier, the IRS allows you to file for an automatic extension of time to file, giving you up to October 15 to file your return. However, you must still pay the tax by April 15. There is an exception to the late payment penalty if you paid at least 90% of the ultimate tax owed by April 15.

If both the late payment and late filing penalties apply, the 0.5% penalty for late payment (but not the 1% penalty for continued nonpayment) will offset the penalty for late filing, during the period that the penalties run concurrently.

6.2 Canada

If you have a balance owing, CRA will charge compound daily interest on any unpaid amounts owing. In addition, CRA will charge interest on the penalties starting the day after your return is due. The rate of interest can change as often as every three months.

If you owe tax and do not file your return on time, CRA will charge you a late-filing penalty. The penalty is 5% of your balance owing, plus 1% of your balance owing for each full month your return is late, up to a maximum of 12 months.

If CRA charged a late-filing penalty on your return for any of the previous three years, your late-filing penalty may be 10%, plus 2% of the balance owing for each full month your return is late, to a maximum of 20 months.

If you failed to report an amount on your current return and you also failed to report an amount on your return for the previous three years, you may have to pay a federal and provincial/territorial repeated failure to report income penalty. The federal and provincial/territorial penalties are each 10% of the amount that you failed to report on your return for the current year.

7. Filing Status

There are five filing statuses in the US: single, married filing jointly, married filing separately, head of household, and qualifying widow or widower.

In Canada, couples file their own separate returns; in the US married couples can, and typically do, file a joint return where both spouses report all of their income and deductions on a single return. Married couples may choose to file separately, but not as singles.

While it is usually beneficial for married couples to file jointly in the US, there can be circumstances where filing separately might be beneficial. The most common situation in which a couple might consider filing separately is when one spouse has many more deductible expenses than the other spouse, such as medical expenses where the deduction is limited to the amount that exceeds 7.5% of income.

> Example: Jane is a US resident. She has an income of $100,000 and her husband Bob has an income of $30,000. Bob also had $10,000 of medical expenses, whereas Jane had no medical expenses. If Jane and Bob were to file jointly, they would have $130,000 of income and their medical expenses would be limited to $250, the amount above 7.5% of $130,000 ($130,000 x 7.5% = $9,750). In other words, the first $9,750 would not be deductible. On the other hand, if they filed separately, Bob would be allowed to deduct $7,750, as only $2,250 would not be allowed ($30,000 x 7.5% = $2,250).

8. Address Changes

8.1 Notifying the IRS when you have a change of address

The IRS will send all correspondence to your last known address. This includes any claims of refund or deficiency notices. Keeping the IRS up to date on how to get a hold of you is important because your refund may be delayed otherwise. If you owe the IRS money, simply changing your address and not telling them does not help; the IRS can enforce a deficiency even if you never received the notice, as long as they sent it to your last known address.

To update your address, you can call the IRS at 1-800-829-1040 or file Form 8822, or correct the address on an IRS correspondence and sending it back to the IRS with the correct information. We recommend filing the form rather than calling, since the 800 number above is the general number and you may be on hold for a long time. When filing Form 8822, we recommend you send it by registered mail so that you have proof it was sent and received.

If you are sending Form 8822 from Canada, mail to:

Department of the Treasury
Internal Revenue Service
Austin, TX 73301-0023
USA

8.2 Notifying CRA when you have a change of address

You can update your address with CRA online at www.cra.gc.ca/myaccount, or by completing Form RC325. If you are completing Form RC325, mail to your local office listed below:

Jonquil Tax Centre	Shawinigan-Sud Tax Centre
PO Box 1900 Stn LCD	PO Box 3000 Stn Main
Jonquil QC	Shawinigan-Sud QC
G7S 5J1	G9N 7S6
St. John's Tax Centre	Sudbury Tax Centre
PO Box 12071 Stn A	PO Box 20000 Stn A
St. John's NL	Sudbury ON
A1B 3Z1	P3A 5C1
Summerside Tax Centre	Surrey Tax Centre
102 – 275 Pope Road	9755 King George Boulevard
Summerside PE	Surrey BC
C1N 5Z7	V3T 5E1
Winnipeg Tax Centre	International Tax Services Office
PO Box 14005 Stn Main	PO Box 9769 Stn T
Winnipeg MB	Ottawa ON
R3C 0E3	K1G 3Y4

9. Overview of Entity Taxation and Rates

In Canada, individuals, corporations, and certain trusts are subject to income tax. In general, partnerships are treated the same in Canada as they are in the US, but corporations and trusts are treated differently.

9.1 Partnerships

Partnerships flow the profits and losses through to the partners, and are not themselves taxed. Partnerships are called "flow-through" entities. This means that the income, expenses, and ultimately the income tax flows through to the individual partners. In the US, partnerships must file Form 1065 and partners receive a form called Schedule K-1 which reports their share of income, deductions, etc. In Canada, Form T5013 must be filed; copies of the forms are given to the partners to report their share of the partnership income and expenses.

9.2 Limited Liability Companies

A US Limited Liability Company (LLC) is a hybrid entity in the US; it can be treated as a corporation, partnership, or sole practitioner. However, in Canada, an LLC is always treated as a corporation, regardless of how it is treated in the US. Do not use an LLC as a resident of Canada because Canada treats an LLC like a corporation, thereby causing double tax.

9.3 Trusts

There are two broad categories of trusts; testamentary (created at death) or inter vivos (created during life) and each type has different tax rules. The inter vivos trust is a separate tax-paying entity, but in some circumstances trust income can be allocated to the beneficiaries and taxed at the individual level. The inter vivos trust does not have graduated tax rates, the trust pays tax at the top individual tax rate. The testamentary trust uses the individual graduated tax rates and can have a tax year-end other than a calendar year-end. To prevent an indefinite capital gains deferral, Canada deems the trust to dispose of its assets every 21 years. An exception exists for spousal trusts, in which case the deemed disposition will be deemed to occur upon the spouse's death.

9.4 Corporations

In Canada, corporations are a very popular entity used for asset protection and tax planning, so we will spend a fair amount of time reviewing corporations.

A Canadian corporation allows for lower tax rates for small-business corporations that are Canadian-controlled, also referred to as Canadian-Controlled Private Corporations (CCPCs). To be Canadian-controlled, 90% or more of the fair market value of its assets must be used in an active business carried on at least 50% in Canada. The second thing that makes Canadian corporations different is that, unlike in the US, income earned in a Canadian corporation is not double taxed.

Generally, a CCPC that earns less than $500,000 CAD (threshold is less in some provinces) in revenue each year is considered a "small corporation." If the corporation is owned primarily by Canadians (Canadian-controlled), the corporation pays a maximum of 10.5% federal tax (plus provincial tax ranging from 0 to 8%), for a total tax of 10.5% to 18.5%. If the corporate revenue exceeds $500,000, then the rates vary from 27% to 31%. Corporate rates are substantially lower than individual tax rates which vary from approximately as much as 40 to 55%, depending on the province in which you live. In Canada, earning income in a corporation allows for significant tax deferral because of the rate differential. Form T2 is the corporate tax form to file in Canada. In the US it is Form 1120.

For 2016, a tax abatement is applied to the basic corporate tax rate of 38%, which brings the corporate tax down to 28%. The federal tax abatement is designed to help offset the provincial tax. From the 28% tax rate, a small-business deduction of 17.5% is allowed for the first $500,000 CAD of active business income, which reduces the federal corporate tax rate 10.5%. As can be seen in Table 3, the federal corporate rate for CCPCs is projected to decrease to 9.0% by 2019.

Table 3
CANADIAN CORPORATE TAX RATES*

Canadian Corporate Tax Rates	2015	2016	2017	2018	2019+
Basic tax	38.0%	38.0%	38.0%	38.0%	38.0%
Federal tax abatement	-10.0%	-10.0%	-10.0%	-10.0%	-10.0%
Small business deduction	-17.0%	-17.5%	-18.0%	-18.5%	-19.0%
Reduced corporate rate	11.0%	10.5%	10.0%	9.5%	9.0%

*Per the 2015 federal budget

The US has two basic types of corporations, a "C" corporation and an "S" corporation. The C corporation is the original (traditional) and the S corporation refers to a subsection of the Internal Revenue Code that allows the shareholders to elect to have the income and expenses flow through to the shareholders. From a tax perspective, the effect of the election make the S corporation more like a partnership than a corporation. However, not all corporations can make the S election. To be eligible for the S election, the corporation must have 100 or fewer shareholders and the shareholders must be US citizens or US residents.

There are two theories on the appropriate tax treatment of corporations in the US; the entity view and the integration view. The entity view holds that corporations have a perpetual life of their own, that they are independent of their shareholders, and that they are legal entities. As such, they should pay tax separately on their own. This is the US perspective.

The integration view holds that the taxation of business income from corporations is viewed as simply the legal form through which one or more individuals carry on business. Therefore, business income that flows through a corporation to an individual should not be taxed differently, in total, from business income earned directly by that individual as a proprietor or partner. This is the Canadian perspective.

Because individual tax rates are higher than corporate tax rates, the dividends paid to individuals are "grossed up" to accomplish approximately the same level of taxation. Currently the gross-up is 38% for eligible dividends. An eligible dividend is a taxable dividend that has been designated as such by the paying corporation. Though some exceptions exist, think of eligible dividends as being paid by public companies.

Average corporate tax rate	27.53623%
Corporate profits	$100,000.00
Corporate tax	$27,536.23
Dividend paid from after-tax profits	$72,463.77
38% gross up	$27,536.23
Taxable dividend to individual	$100,000.00

The gross-up for non-eligible dividends is 17% in 2016, down from 18% in 2015.

Individuals are subject to federal graduated tax rates from 15% to 33%, for 2016:

- 15% on the first $45,282 of taxable income.

- 20.5% on the next $45,281 of taxable income (on the portion of taxable income from $45,282 to $90,563).

- 26% on the next $49,825 of taxable income (on the portion of taxable income from $90,563 to $140,388).

- 29% on the next $59,612 of taxable income (on the portion of taxable income from $140,388 to $200,000).

- 33% on the amount over $200,000.

Federal and many provincial tax rates are graduated, meaning that at higher levels of income you pay progressively higher levels of tax. The tax rate that corresponds to your highest level of income is known as your marginal tax rate.

10. Carrying Charges

Carrying charges in Canada are similar to miscellaneous itemized deductions in the US. You can claim the following carrying charges you paid to earn income from investments —

- fees to manage or take care of your investments (other than administration fees you paid for your Registered Retirement Savings Plan or Registered Retirement Income Fund);

- fees for certain investment advice or for recording investment income;

- fees to have someone complete your return, but only if:
  - you have income from a business or property;
  - accounting is a usual part of the operations of your business or property; and
  - you did not use the amounts claimed to reduce the business or property income you reported;
- most interest you pay on money you borrow for investment purposes, but generally only if you use it to try to earn investment income, including interest and dividends. However, if the only earnings your investment can produce are capital gains, you cannot claim the interest you paid;
- interest you paid on a policy loan made to earn income; and
- legal fees you incurred relating to support payments that your current or former spouse or common-law partner, or the natural parent of your child, will have to pay to you.

You can also deduct your expenses in the following situations:

- You collected late support payments.
- You established the amount of support payments from your current or former spouse or common-law partner.
- You established the amount of support payments from the natural parent of your child (who is not your current or former spouse or common-law partner) where the support is payable under the terms of an order.
- You sought to obtain an increase in support payments.

11. Alternative Minimum Tax

Both the US and Canada have an Alternative Minimum Tax (AMT) that limits the tax advantage you can receive from certain tax incentives. You pay the minimum tax if it is more than the federal tax calculated in the usual way.

11.1 Canadian Alternative Minimum Tax

Some items that affect AMT in Canada are:

- Taxable capital gains
- Loss resulting from, or increased by, claiming capital cost allowance on rental properties
- Loss on a limited partnership

Table 4
TAX RATES FOR CANADIAN-CONTROLLED PRIVATE CORPORATIONS

2016 Corporate Income Tax Rates				
	Active Business Income			
	General	Small Business (CCPC)	Business Limit	Investment Income
Federal	15.0%	10.5%	$500,000	34.7%
Alberta	12.0%	3.0%	$500,000	12.0%
British Columbia	11.0%	2.5%	$500,000	11.0%
Manitoba	12.0%	0%	$450,000	12.0%
New Brunswick	12.0%	4.0%	$500,000	12.0%
Newfoundland & Labrador	14.0%	3.0%	$500,000	14.0%
Nova Scotia	16.0%	3.0%	$350,000	16.0%
Northwest Territories	11.5%	4.0%	$500,000	11.5%
Nunavut	12.0%	4.0%	$500,000	12.0%
Ontario	11.5%	4.5%	$500,000	11.5%
Prince Edward Island	16.0%	4.5%	$500,000	16.0%
Quebec	11.9%	8.0%	$500,000	11.9%
Saskatchewan	12.0%	2.0%	$500,000	12.0%
Yukon	15.0%	3.0%	$500,000	15.0%

- Most carrying charges
- Investment tax credit
- Federal dividend tax credit

The AMT is calculated on Form T691 — Alternative Minimum Tax.

11.2 US Alternative Minimum Tax

To the extent US Alternative Minimum Tax (AMT) exceeds regular federal income tax, a future credit is provided which can offset future regular tax to the extent AMT does not apply in a future year.

AMT does not allow deductions for personal exemptions or the standard deduction. State, local, and foreign taxes are also not deductible.

Table 5
COMBINED MAXIMUM PERSONAL TAX RATES 2016

	Ordinary Income	Capital Gains	Canadian Dividends Eligible	Canadian Dividends Non-eligible
Federal	33.00%	16.50%	24.81%	26.30%
Alberta	48.00%	24.00%	26.30%	31.71%
British Columbia	47.70%	23.85%	31.30%	40.40%
Manitoba	50.40%	25.20%	37.78%	45.69%
New Brunswick	58.75%	29.38%	43.79%	51.75%
Newfoundland and Labrador	48.30%	24.15%	38.47%	39.40%
Northwest Territories	47.05%	23.53%	28.33%	35.72%
Nova Scotia	54.00%	27.00%	41.58%	46.97%
Nunavut	44.50%	22.25%	33.08%	36.35%
Ontario	53.53%	26.76%	39.34%	45.30%
Prince Edward Island	51.37%	25.69%	34.22%	43.87%
Quebec	53.31%	26.69%	39.83%	43.84%
Saskatchewan	48.00%	24.00%	30.33%	40.06%
Yukon	48.00%	24.00%	24.81%	40.18%

You must file Form 6251 if there is any net AMT due. The form is also filed to claim the credit for prior year AMT. Some other individual adjustments in computing AMT include:

- Miscellaneous itemized deductions are not allowed. These include all items subject to the 2% "floor," such as employee business expenses, tax preparation fees, etc.

- The home mortgage interest deduction is limited to interest on purchase money mortgages for a first and second residence.

- Medical expenses may be deducted only if they exceed 10% of Adjusted Gross Income, as compared to 7.5% for regular tax.

12. Residency

One of the most important things you need to know is the rules around when you become a Canadian resident. Since the Canadian tax system is based on

Table 6
PROVINCIAL/TERRITORIAL TAX RATES FOR 2016

Provinces/territories	Rate(s)
Newfoundland and Labrador	7.7% on the first $35,148 of taxable income, + 12.5% on the next $35,147, + 13.3% on next $55,205, + 14.3% on the next $50,200, + 15.3% on the amount over $175,700 **Maximum combined rate is 48.30%**
Prince Edward Island	9.8% on the first $31,984 of taxable income, + 13.8% on the next $31,985, + 16.7% on the amount over $63,969 Plus a Surtax of 10% **Maximum combined rate is 51.37%**
Nova Scotia	8.79% on the first $29,590 of taxable income, + 14.95% on the next $29,590, + 16.67% on the next $33,820, + 17.50% on the next $57,000, + 21.00% on the amount over $150,000 **Maximum combined rate is 54.0%**
New Brunswick	9.68% on the first $40,492 of taxable income, + 14.82% on the next $40,493, + 16.52% on the next $50,679, + 17.84% on the next $18,336, + 21.00% on the next $100,000, + 25.75% on the amount over $250,000 **Maximum combined rate is 58.75%**
Quebec	16.00% on the first $42,390 of taxable income, + 20.00% on the next $42,390, + 24.00% on the next $18,370, + 25.75% on the amount over $103,150 **Maximum combined rate is 53.31%**
Ontario	5.05% on the first $41,536 of taxable income, + 9.15% on the next $41,539, + 11.16% on the next $66,925, + 12.16% on the next $70,000 13.16% on the amount over $220,000 Plus Surtax up to 56% **Maximum combined rate is 53.53%**

Table 6 — Continued

Manitoba	10.80% on the first $31,000 of taxable income, + 12.75% on the next $36,000, + 17.40% on the amount over $67,000 **Maximum combined rate is 50.40%**
Saskatchewan	11.0% on the first $44,601 of taxable income, + 13.0% on the next $82,829, + 15.0% on the amount over $127,430 **Maximum combined rate is 48.0%**
Alberta	10% on the first $125,000 of taxable income, + 12% on the next $25,000, + 13% on the next $50,000, + 14% on the next $100,000, + 15% on the amount over $300,000 **Maximum combined rate is 48.0%**
British Columbia	5.06% on the first $38,210 of taxable income, + 7.70% on the next $38,211, + 10.50% on the next $11,320, + 12.29% on the next $18,802, + 14.70% on the amount over $106,543 **Maximum combined rate is 47.70%**
Yukon	6.04% on the first $45,282 of taxable income, + 9.00% on the next $45,281, + 10.90% on the next $49,825, + 12.80% on the next $359,612 + 15.00% on the amount over $500,000 Plus a Surtax of 5% **Maximum combined rate is 48%**
Northwest Territories	5.90% on the first $41,011 of taxable income, + 8.60% on the next $41,013, + 12.20% on the next $51,329, + 14.05% on the amount over $133,353 **Maximum combined rate is 47.05%**
Nunavut	4.0% on the first $43,176 of taxable income, + 7.0% on the next $43,175, + 9.0% on the next $54,037, + 11.5% on the amount over $140,388 **Maximum combined rate is 44.50%**

Table 7
CANADIAN FEDERAL INDIVIDUAL TAX CALCULATION

	Worldwide income from employment, business, property, and all other non-capital sources (only positive amounts are added here)
Plus	Net capital gains (capital gains minus capital losses)
Minus	Deductions
Minus	Losses from employment, business, property (capital losses), and business investment losses
Equals	Net Income for Tax Purposes
Minus	Division C (Other) Deductions
Equals	Taxable Income
Times	Progressive Tax Rates
Equals	Federal Tax before Credits
Minus	Non-Refundable and Refundable Tax Credits
Equals	Federal Tax Payable

residency, as we discussed previously, you need to understand when you are a resident and when you are not. Determining residency status is not as straightforward as you would think.

To begin with, an individual's residency status is determined on a case-by-case basis and the individual's whole situation and all relevant facts must be considered. In other words, there is no clear line and in fact there may be more than one day that can be argued as the day your residency in Canada began.

The government may lead you to believe that if you apply this or that test, then voila, you have the answer. Regardless of what the government may believe or want, the answer is not always that clear. There is a fair amount of ambiguity that you can use when planning your entry into or out of Canada.

The relevant facts in determining your residency status include the residential ties you have in Canada, the purpose and permanence of your stays abroad, and your ties abroad. The following steps can help you determine your residency status for income tax purposes and your tax obligations to Canada.

12.1 Step 1: Determine if you have residential ties with Canada

The most important thing to consider when determining your residency status in Canada for income tax purposes is whether or not you maintain, or you establish, residential ties with Canada. Think of your residential ties as weights being placed on a scale where not all items weigh the same and none of them, by themselves, can determine residency.

Significant residential ties to Canada include:

- a home in Canada,

- a spouse or common-law partner in Canada, and

- dependents in Canada.

Secondary residential ties that may be relevant include:

- personal property in Canada, such as a car or furniture,

- social ties in Canada, such as memberships in Canadian recreational or religious organizations,

- economic ties in Canada, such as Canadian bank accounts or credit cards,

- a Canadian driver's license,

- a Canadian passport, and

- health insurance with a Canadian province or territory.

Note that the residential ties you establish or maintain in other countries may also be relevant.

12.2 Step 2: Determine your residency status and its tax implications

Your residency status if you entered Canada:

- When you leave the US (or any other country) to settle in Canada and you establish significant residential ties and became a resident of Canada in the tax year, you may be considered an immigrant.

- If you have ties in the US (or any other country) that Canada has a tax treaty with and you are considered to be a resident of that country, but you are also a factual resident of Canada because you established significant residential ties with Canada, you may be considered a deemed nonresident of Canada.

- If you have not established significant residential ties with Canada to be considered a factual resident, but you stayed in Canada for 183 or more days in the year, you may be considered a deemed resident of Canada.

Your residency status if you normally, customarily, or routinely live in another country:

- If you did not have significant residential ties with Canada and you lived outside Canada throughout the year (except if you were a deemed resident of Canada), you may be considered a nonresident of Canada.

- If you did not have significant residential ties with Canada and you stayed in Canada for less than 183 days in the tax year, you may be considered a nonresident of Canada.

If you want the CRA's opinion on your residency status, complete Form NR74, Determination of Residency Status (Entering Canada) and send it to the International and Ottawa Tax Services Office.

Note: We highly recommend that you consult with an experienced tax professional on this issue. Do not rely on what CRA tells you; in fact, don't even call them. The reasons not to call the CRA or the IRS are: 1) the person you would talk to will likely not know the answer, 2) they are not responsible for any bad or incorrect advice they provide, and 3) many issues have two sides to them, but the government will always provide you with the government line, which is never to your benefit.

13. Tax Audits and Dealing with the CRA

The CRA selects returns to audit based on a risk assessment that looks at such things as number of errors on a return, "indications of non-compliance," and a comparison of information from other sources to determine if your return should be audited.

One thing that is a little different in Canada is that not only are your personal records subject to audit, but your business records, or records of other individuals or entities, are considered part of the items that relate, or may relate, to the tax return being examined by the CRA. This means among other things that the CRA can examine the records of your family members and ask questions of your employees.

According to an article called "7 triggers that may lead to a tax audit" published in the *Toronto Star* on May 19, 2013, there are seven factors that will possibly trigger a CRA audit:

1. Being self-employed.

2. Big changes.

3. Recurring losses.

4. Big expenses.

5. Not blending in (having similar income and expenses as others in your situation).

6. Aggressive tax planning.

7. Home office expenses.

13.1 The CRA examination (audit) process

The CRA examines (audits) tax returns to verify that the tax reported is correct. Selecting a return for examination does not always suggest that the taxpayer has either made an error or been dishonest. In fact, some examinations result in a refund to the taxpayer or acceptance of the return without change.

The CRA selects returns for examination using a variety of methods, including:

- **Audit projects:** In some cases, the CRA will test the compliance of a particular group of taxpayers. If the test results indicate that there is significant noncompliance within the group, CRA may audit based on a local, regional, or national basis.

- **Computer-generated list:** Most returns are selected for review from computer-generated lists. For example, the computer system can compare selected financial information of taxpayers engaged in similar businesses or occupations and generate lists of returns with audit potential. From these lists, CRA will choose specific returns to be audited.

- **Leads:** Leads include information from other audits or investigations, as well as information from outside sources.

- **Related examinations:** Sometimes CRA will select files for audit because of their association with other related audits. For example, if you are in partnership with another taxpayer, and that person's file has been selected for audit, it is usually more convenient to examine all of the records at the same time.

An examination may be conducted by mail or through an in-person interview and review of the taxpayer's records. The interview may be at a CRA office (office audit) or at the taxpayer's home, place of business, or accountant's office (field audit).

Note: Do not attempt to handle a CRA or IRS audit on your own; hire an experienced and competent tax professional to represent you.

14. Dealing with the CRA

While the CRA has a much better reputation than the IRS as far as being friendly, in many important ways the CRA is more difficult to deal with. The number one problem is that on average the CRA is slower to respond to inquiries or to settle a dispute. One extreme example occurred a number of years ago, where CRA was telling a taxpayer that the withholding on his military pension should have been 25% because it was a lump-sum withdrawal. It took us nearly four years to get someone at the CRA to realize that a lump-sum withdrawal from a military pension was impossible. At least they were pleasant to work with the entire time.

The other big problem that arises from time-to-time is that (in our experience) some people at the CRA have a notion of what they believe should be the correct answer, without regard to what the law actually is. At least twice, when we were appealing a client's Notice of Assessment, the person from the CRA explicitly said he did not care what the law was. At least when we are appealing a case with the IRS, the argument is over the correct interpretation of the law, not what someone's opinion is.

In the US you are typically not be contacted by the IRS unless they want something, such as additional information. However, in Canada, you will receive a Notice of Assessment after you file your return. This is not something to worry about, in fact, it is something you should look forward to. The notice will tell you that CRA has reviewed your return and has accepted it as filed or they have additional questions. Either way, you do not have to wait and hope no news is good news like you do in the US.

Caution: One thing to point out is that Canadians seem to be much more likely to call Canada Revenue Agency (CRA) or the IRS to ask questions about the law than Americans are. We suggest that you do not call CRA or the IRS for advice for a number of reasons. First and most important is that neither the CRA nor the IRS is bound by the advice they provide on the phone. In the best of cases, you are flipping a coin as to whether you will get an answer that is correct. Given that you will have a number of cross-border issues, this will increase the complexity and therefore decrease the likelihood of receiving an answer you can rely on. We recommend that you do not bet thousands of dollars on whether you have been given a correct answer. Second, when talking to the CRA or IRS agent, you may not accurately convey the issue or you may not understand the answer due to the fact that you do not understand the law or the tax lexicon. Lastly, you may inadvertently tell the CRA or the IRS agent something you should not.

4

The Treaty

Cross-border tax and financial planners have the complex task of understanding three distinct tax and legal regimes and how they interact with each other:

- the laws of the United States of America,
- the laws of Canada, and
- the laws of the Canada-US Tax Treaty.

1. History of the Canada-US Tax Treaty

Canada was America's first treaty partner when, in 1936, The Reciprocal Tax Convention came into force. The Reciprocal Tax Convention was in effect until 1941, when it was replaced by The Canada-US Tax Convention. The current Treaty was signed on September 26, 1980 and has subsequently been amended by five protocols. The most recent became effective January 1, 2009.

The Treaty is frequently presented in its 1980 version, with protocols having to be read separately, so you must be cautious that you are reading the latest version of the Treaty.

There is a supplement to the Treaty called the Income Tax Conventions Interpretation Act (ITCIA) that defines terms within the Treaty. The most common example is the definition of "periodic," as in periodic payments. The Treaty simply states that a periodic payment is subject to 15% withholding. The Treaty does not define what a periodic payment is; you must go to the ITCIA to find the definition.

1.1 The relationship of the "laws of the land" to the Treaty

In Canada, the Treaty generally forms part of the law of Canada upon enactment and subject to the provisions of the Income Tax Conventions Interpretation Act (ITCIA), the Treaty prevails over the *Income Tax Act*, only to the extent of inconsistency.

Under American law, the Constitution treats tax treaties on equal footing with US domestic law; both are "the supreme law of the land." A longstanding principle of American jurisprudence has been that if a treaty conflicts with a federal law, the latter (whichever came later in time) will prevail.

2. Treaty Overview

The Canada-US Treaty is formally known as "The Convention between Canada and the United States of America with Respect to Taxes on Income and Capital" (referred to as the Treaty) and exists primarily to prevent the same income being taxed by more than one country (double taxation). This can occur whenever you are a resident of one country and earn income in another country; for example, you are living in Canada and have interest, dividend, and pension income from the US. These situations create a potential for double taxation because your country of residence, Canada, and the US have the right to tax the same income.

The Treaty also aids in the enforcement of the countries' tax laws by providing for exchanges of information between the different tax authorities, and in some cases requires the other country to assist in the collection of tax due it. For example, if you owe the IRS money and move to Canada, in some cases CRA will be bound by the Treaty to assist in the collection efforts of the IRS, and vice versa.

Tax treaties include procedures for resolving differences of opinion between the countries on questions such as the taxation of a specific item of income, which country the income was earned in, or the tax residency of the taxpayer. In the Treaty, this is referred to as sending the issue to "competent authority." This means that the issue gets sent to the legal departments of CRA and the Internal Revenue Agency where they decide who has the right to tax the individual or company. The result could be more significant than simply knowing who to write the check to; the decision could result in higher tax if one country was able to tax the income versus the other country.

Tax treaties are increasingly important in this era of increased globalization. Treaties provide dependable answers as to which country has the right to tax businesses that operate or invest abroad, new ventures that seek foreign investment, and individuals who want to live or work in another country.

Note: There have been five protocol amendments over the years. The time between when the amendments are negotiated and signed, and when they are ratified by the respective governments can be significant. This difference in time can cause planning nightmares, as happened with the latest (fifth) protocol when 15 months passed between it being signed and the governments ratifying it.

The Treaty is based on the model developed by the Organization of Economic Cooperation and Development (OECD), but also includes some features that are unique to the Canada-US relationship. As cross-border situations evolve, the Treaty must also evolve to remain effective. As mentioned, the Treaty has been updated five times, in 1983, 1984, 1995, 1997 and 2009. These changes to the Treaty, known as protocols, ensure the Treaty has adapted to the latest tax developments in each country, as well as the changing needs of Canadian and US individuals and businesses.

3. Inside the Treaty

The discussion in this chapter is not a technical interpretation of the Treaty; it is also not meant to be all-encompassing, but rather to make you aware of some of the Articles (Chapters) of the Treaty that relate to Americans living in Canada.

The Treaty applies to residents of Canada and the US and applies to all taxes imposed under the *Income Tax Act* of Canada and to the income and estate taxes imposed by the US Internal Revenue Code. The Treaty also applies to the US accumulated earnings tax, personal holding company tax, US excise tax on private foundations, and social security taxes. The estate tax was not included until the third protocol (1995) provided that the Treaty also include US estate taxes imposed by the Internal Revenue Code.

Taxes imposed by the provinces in Canada and by the states of the US are not covered by the Treaty. In the US, each state has its own tax laws and some of the states will not directly accept the provisions of the Canada-US Tax Convention, but will indirectly accept them because their tax laws use, as the starting point for tax computation, federal adjusted gross income. Since the starting point is federal adjusted gross income, any income or exclusion for US purposes will be allowed for state income tax purposes, unless otherwise specifically noted; one such state is Arizona. Some states do not accept the provisions of the Treaty because they have their own systems of computing income; one such state is California. Some states, such as Michigan, accept taxes paid to a Canadian province as credits against their state tax.

Important: The point made above about some states indirectly allowing for the benefits of the Treaty and some not, is very important. One example that will be discussed in more detail in Chapter 6 is the taxation of RRSPs by Arizona and California. The Treaty allows the annual earnings of RRSPs to be deferred. In a state like Arizona, the deferral is not part of the federal adjusted gross income so the income will not be included in Arizona and thus will also be deferred in Arizona. However, since the deferral has no effect in California, the annual earnings within your RRSP will be taxed if you live in California (even if you make no withdrawals). The only ways around this issue are to not live in a state like California or to cash out your RRSPs.

We will not discuss all of the Articles in this book, but many of these topics have additional detail in other chapters. For example, dividends and interest will also be discussed in Chapter 7 on Investing in Canada.

3.1 Saving clause

Before we started talking about how the different sections of the Treaty affect you, beware that these general rules may be overridden by the "Savings Clause." The clause (Article XXIX, Miscellaneous Rules) preserves the right of each country to tax its own residents as if no tax treaty were in effect. Thus, once you become a resident of Canada, you will be subject to Canadian tax on your worldwide income, yet as a US citizen you will also be subject to US tax on your worldwide income. The saving clause may prohibit you from claiming certain treaty benefits because you are a US citizen. One example is that capital gains are generally taxable only in the country of residence. However, a US citizen living in Canada will still have to report all capital gains on a US tax return. However, as you will see in Chapter 5 on Foreign Tax Credits, you will generally not be subject to double tax.

3.2 Disclosing treaty benefits claimed

If you claim treaty benefits that override or modify any provision of the Internal Revenue Code, and by claiming these benefits your tax is or might be reduced, you must attach a fully completed Form 8833 — Treaty-Based Return Position Disclosure to your tax return. There are similar forms in Canada for reporting treaty benefits; Forms NR301, 302, and 303.

4. Residency

An individual or an entity such as a corporation or partnership is considered to be resident of a country if it is the individual's or entity's country of domicile, residence, place of management, place of incorporation, or other criteria of a similar nature. If you or an entity of yours is considered a resident, you and/or that entity will be subject to the taxes of that country, therefore it is very important to know of which country you and your entity are resident.

Note: If you are a Lawful Permanent Resident of the US (green card holder), who has not formally surrendered your green card, you are considered a US resident and must report and pay tax on your worldwide income. See Chapter 11 on Tax for Americans Living in Canada, for more details.

US citizens are always taxed on their worldwide income, regardless of where they actually reside. US citizens who reside in Canada will also be taxed as Canadian residents, under the laws of Canada.

It is possible that if you spend time and have activities in both Canada and the US, your tax residency may be in question. When an individual's residency status is questioned, the Treaty has "tie-breaker" rules with which to settle the issue. Refer back to Chapters 1 and 3 for more about establishing residency.

The tie-breaker rules provide four questions for you to answer. If the answer to the first question does not decide which country you are a resident of, go on to the next question, and so on until you can determine which country you are a resident of. Once you get a clear answer, stop, that is where you are a resident. The questions are:

1. Where is your permanent home?

2. Where are your closest economic and personal relations?

3. Where is your "habitual abode" (the country where you spend most of your time)?

4. Of what country are you a citizen?

If, after answering these four questions, you cannot determine where you are considered a resident, then you can request that the competent authorities of Canada and the US settle the issue by Mutual Agreement. What this means is that CRA and the IRS will get together and decide.

Businesses that operate on both sides of the border need to understand in which jurisdiction they will be taxed on their profits. The concept of "Permanent Establishment" is defined in the Treaty to determine which country has the right to tax the profits of the business. A permanent establishment for businesses is analogous to residency for individuals. For example, the profits of a business resident in Canada would be taxable in the US only to the extent that some or all of the profits are attributable to a permanent establishment in the US. A permanent establishment would include the following:

1. a place of management;

2. a branch;

3. an office;

4. a factory:

5. a workshop;

6. a mine, oil or gas well, a quarry, or other place of resource extraction;

7. a building or construction site that lasts more than 12 months; and

8. a person acting on behalf of the resident of the other country if they have the authority to conclude contracts (not including independent agents).

A permanent establishment would not include a facility solely for storage or warehousing, distribution, research, or advertising. It would also not include a business that uses a broker or independent agent. A permanent establishment can also occur when a business in one country sends an employee to work in the other country for more than 182 days in any 12-month period, and more than 50% of the revenues of the business are derived from the services provided in the other country.

If there is a permanent establishment in the other country then the Treaty will tax the business profits as if the permanent establishment were a distinct and separate entity. That means only the revenues generated and expenses incurred in that permanent establishment would determine the profits that would be subject to tax in the other country. Said another way, if you have a Canadian business with a permanent establishment in the US, the entire profits will not be taxable in the US. Additionally the Treaty allows for the allocation of certain head office expenses, such as general administrative expenses, that would be allocable to the permanent establishment even though the expense was incurred in the other country. The domestic tax rules of each country include the application of foreign tax credits, which is a mechanism to eliminate double tax. To take this example one step further, if you have a business in Canada that had a permanent establishment in the US, the US would tax the profits on the US operations only and Canada would tax the profits on the worldwide profits. The company would be allowed a foreign tax credit for the taxes paid to the US so that in the end, the tax paid in Canada, after credits, is only the tax on the Canadian profits.

5. Real Property

The Treaty directs that income derived from real property (real estate) situated in the other country may be taxed in the other country. Any rental income from the use of real property is taxed in the country where the property is located. Any sale of real property is also taxed in the country where the real property is located. As an example, if when you moved to Canada you did not sell your US home and you decided to rent the US home while you are living in Canada, the profit on the rental income will be fully taxable in the US and Canada. Any income tax you pay in the US can be taken as a foreign tax credit on your Canadian tax return. When you decide to sell your home, the same idea applies: You will be taxed in Canada and the US on the profit, and a foreign tax credit is taken on the Canadian return to prevent double taxation.

Important: The *Income Tax Act* allows you an unlimited exemption for gain on your principal residence, however any gain that occurs after the home is no longer your principal residence is taxable upon sale. The problem is that when it comes time to sell your home in the future, how do you determine the amount of gain since the time it was your principal residence? The answer is to get at least one (three would be better) "broker's opinions" as to the value of your home, as close as possible to your date of exit from Canada. The amount up to this value will be tax free as your principal residence; any price received above that amount will be taxable as a capital gain in Canada.

The taxation of a home that was, at some point, used as your principal residence in the US can be significantly different in Canada. The main reason is that while Canada allows for an unlimited exemption of gain, the US allows for $250,000 USD per person ($500,000 USD per couple), if the home was your principal residence at least two out of the previous five years. So one way the taxation could be different is if the gain is greater than the $250,000/$500,000, or the other way it could be different is if you have rented the US home for more than three years after moving to Canada. In this latter case, you would lose the US exemption altogether.

The other way the tax could be different is when there is a change in the value of the currency. You could have no gain or even a loss in the value of the home, but the currency could improve by the time you sell and you would have a gain that would have to be reported. This issue applies to everything, but is most pronounced in real estate because of the time span between purchase and sale, and the dollars involved.

6. Dividends, Interest, and Royalties

Dividends paid by a company in one country to a resident of the other country may be taxed in the other country. In addition, the country from which the payer of the dividend is resident can tax the dividend as well. What this means is that if you are living in Canada and you receive a dividend from a US company, there would normally be withholding in the US and that dividend would have to be included in your Canadian income and taxed accordingly. In every case where income is reported and subject to tax in both countries, a foreign tax credit is available to avoid double tax.

Interest paid by a resident of one country to a resident of the other country after January 1, 2009 will only be taxed in the country of residence. The Fifth Protocol eliminated the nonresident withholding tax on interest, when the interest is paid as part of an arm's length transaction.

Most royalties are exempt from any withholding taxes, such as copyright royalties in respect of the production or reproduction of any literary, dramatic, musical, or artistic work. Royalties from motion pictures and works on film, videotape, or other means of reproduction for use in connection with television are subject to 10% withholding. Royalties for industrial equipment is subject to a 30% withholding.

Caution: If you are a US citizen or green card holder, you are subject to US tax on your worldwide income as if you were a resident of the US. If you recall our discussion of the Savings Clause earlier, US citizens are not subject to the nonresident withholding rules because they are required to file US tax returns the same as American residents would. We will go into much more detail on green card holders living in Canada in Chapter 11, but for now simply follow the same rules as American citizens in filing US tax returns.

7. Gains on Personal Property

The Treaty has different rules if the gain is from real property (real estate) than from all other gains (personal property). Generally, personal property gains are taxable only in the country of residence, whereas gains arising from real property are taxed in the country where the real property is located and in the country of residence, as we have already discussed. For non-US citizens, personal property gains such as those you incur on your investment portfolio are not taxable in the country they occurred; they are taxable only in the country in which you are resident. However, as a US citizen, you will have to report and pay taxes in both countries and use the foreign tax credit to avoid double tax.

The Treaty allows you to step up the basis of your assets when you move to Canada because you are only subject to Canadian tax while you are a resident of Canada. As mentioned in previous chapters, you need to determine and document the value of your capital assets as of the date you became a Canadian taxpayer, and those values will be your Canadian purchase price.

8. Personal Services

Generally, if you are living in Canada and receive employment income (or self-employment income) for services performed in US, the income is exempt from tax in Canada, if the income does not exceed $10,000 in the source country currency. However, for an American citizen living in Canada, this rule does not apply because of the savings clause discussed earlier.

9. Artists and Athletes

Income of an artist or athlete may be taxed in the source country when the gross revenue exceeds $15,000 in the currency of the source country. For example, if you are a musician resident in Canada and you perform a concert in the US and receive more than $15,000 CAD (gross, before expenses), then you must report and pay tax in Canada on all of the income (less expenses). The musician does not simply report the amount above the $15,000 CAD threshold; $15,000 or less is exempt, $15,001 and greater and everything is taxable. The gross receipts would include all expense reimbursements. The US resident musician would also include his or her US receipts and expenses in a Canadian tax return and would receive a credit against any Canadian tax for taxes paid in the US.

An entertainer would include a theater, motion picture, and radio or television artist. In order to qualify as an artist or entertainer the taxpayer must generally "provide the performance that the audience seeks to experience." There was a case in Canada of a "play-by-play" personality who claimed that he was an entertainer, and the court ruled that he was not an artist for purposes of this article of the Treaty, but rather a radio journalist.

The Treaty also treats the income of artists or athletes as being earned by the artist or athlete regardless of whether the income is earned directly or indirectly through some type of entity, such as a corporation. Therefore, if in the example above, the US resident musician earned the income from a concert in Canada, through a corporation, then the corporation would pay tax in Canada on the income earned in Canada.

These rules do not apply to the athlete who is employed by a team that participates in a league, such as the National Hockey League or Major League Baseball. Therefore, a US resident hockey player who earns a salary from a US hockey team would be exempt from Canadian taxation if he was not present in Canada for more than 182 days in any 12-month period, his remuneration was not borne by a team in Canada, and the team did not have a permanent establishment in Canada (or the income earned was less than $10,000 CAD).

10. Pensions and Annuities

An important article of the Treaty that interests many seniors deals with pensions and annuities. The tax treatment of pensions and annuities in one country is respected by the other country. This means that if you receive a pension or annuity in the US that is partially taxable and partially tax-free, Canada will treat it the same way. Monthly payments from company or government pensions and annuities are subject to a 15% nonresident withholding tax. The term pension, as it is used in the Treaty, means a company or government retirement benefit for employment services performed. The Treaty defines an annuity as "a stated sum paid periodically at stated times during the life or during a specified number of years, under an obligation to make payments ... "

Though the Treaty treats IRAs (including Roth IRAs) and RRSPs as pensions, Registered Savings plans are taxed differently than company and government pensions and annuities. Withdrawals from an RRSP are always considered a lump-sum distribution and subject to 25% withholding. Withdrawals from an RRIF can be either a lump-sum or periodic. Lump-sum distributions are subject to 25% withholding and periodic payments are subject to 15% withholding. A periodic distribution has a specific definition; the lesser of 10% of the beginning of the year value, or twice the required minimum distribution. Registered savings plans have special reporting requirements in the US, whereas a pension generally does not.

US retirement accounts can generally be broken down into employer-sponsored plans such as 401(k), 403(b), profit sharing plans and defined benefit retirement plans, and Individual Retirement Accounts (IRAs), such as a traditional IRA and Roth IRA. There are other types of accounts, but these are the most common and the ones we will discuss. A traditional IRA is analogous to an RRSP; you contribute money to an account you control, up to a certain limit. Contributions up to the limit are tax deductible and continue to be deferred until withdrawn. Minimum payments are required beginning in the year you turn age 70½.

The big difference between RRSPs and IRAs is the contribution limits. For 2016, the contribution limit for an RRSP is $25,370 CAD, while the contribution limit for an IRA is $5,500 USD if you are under the age of 50 and $6,500 USD if age 50 or older. Also, is that while you can carry over any unused RRSP contributions you did not make, in the US there is a use it or lose it rule; you are not able to carry over your unused contributions.

A US Roth IRA is similar to a Canadian Tax Free Savings Account (TFSA), where you receive no deduction for contributions, but the money comes out tax-free. There are three factors to think about when deciding if you should invest in an after-tax program or in a pre-tax program: 1) assumed tax rates during accumulation versus tax rates during draw down, 2) whether you will be able to defer withdrawal past the required distribution age of the pre-tax accounts (longer deferral), and 3) if you are able to invest the time and effort, you may use the after-tax accounts to reduce withdrawals from the pre-tax accounts, and thereby manage your tax brackets.

The Fifth Protocol tried to create parity in the treatment of retirement plans between the US and Canada. A qualified contribution and deduction in one country qualifies as a deduction in the other country, subject to the limits of that country. For example, if a Canadian resident, US citizen contributes more than $5,500 USD/$6,500 USD to his or her RRSP, only the $5,500 or $6,500 will be deductible. Per the Treaty, the plans also retain their tax characteristics in the other country. For example, a Roth IRA continues to be tax-deferred and withdrawals continue to be tax-free for Canadian residents. One exception to this is the TFSA; it is not identified in the Treaty as a "pension" and it is therefore not covered by the Treaty, and by default is taxable in the US.

11. Social Security

Social security benefits paid by Canada in the form of Canada or Quebec Pension Plan (CPP or QPP) and Old Age Security (OAS) and Social Security benefits paid by the US are taxable only in the country of residence. Because the benefits are taxable only in the country of residence, there is no withholding by the country paying the benefits. In the US, your Canadian benefits are taxed the same as US Social Security is taxed in the US. For Americans living in Canada receiving US Social Security, the benefits are only 85% taxable in Canada.

Canadians who attain the age of 65 years are entitled to receive OAS which is based on the number of years after age 18 that the applicant has resided in Canada. In order to receive the full entitlement, the applicant has to have resided in Canada for 20 years after age 18. If you have resided in Canada for at least 10 years after the age of 18, you can still receive an Old Age Security pension if you reside outside Canada.

Note: The US-Canada Agreement on Social Security allows you to count the years you contributed to the US Social Security system, to count as years of residency in Canada for purposes of qualifying for OAS.

See Chapter 6 for more about OAS benefits.

12. Government Service

Employees of foreign governments' earnings are taxable in their home country and/or based on their citizenship. As an example, an employee of a Canadian consulate office in the US would only be taxable as a resident of Canada and would not be taxable in the US provided the employee was also not a US citizen. If the employee was a US citizen, he or she would be taxed in Canada on earnings in Canada as a nonresident of Canada, and would be taxed in the US on that income, and would receive a credit against US taxes for the tax paid to Canada.

13. Students

Under the Treaty, an individual who normally resides in one country and becomes a full-time student, apprentice, or business trainee in the other country would be exempt from tax on payments received from his or her country of residence. A Canadian resident who attends school in the US would be exempt from tax on any amounts received for the student's maintenance, education, or training from Canada. Any income earned by the student in the US through employment would naturally be taxable in the US.

14. Taxes Imposed by Reason of Death

The Treaty includes rules to coordinate the death tax regimes of each country. The US imposes an estate tax at death, which is a tax on the fair market value of assets owned by the decedent (the person who died) at death, whereas Canada imposes an income tax on the accrued gain of assets to the date of death.

We have devoted an entire chapter to taxes at death; see Chapter 10.

One thing that confuses even many professionals is the estate tax exemption allowed to US residents. Residents of the US have the same exemption as US citizens. In 2016, that amount is $5,450,000 USD. The thing US citizens get that non-citizen residents do not is an unlimited marital deduction. This means that if an estate exceeds the exemption, a US citizen can receive an unlimited amount from a deceased spouse, whereas a non-US citizen can only receive the exemption amount tax-free. Nonresidents are generally allowed a $60,000 exemption. The Treaty allows for a pro-rata exemption.

The other important feature of this section of the Treaty provides a tax credit for death taxes paid to the other country. While there are some important exceptions to this credit, (see Chapter 10) generally speaking if you have assets in both countries and death taxes are paid in both countries, there will be a credit allowed for the other country's tax.

The full treaty text can be found at http://laws-lois.justice.gc.ca/eng/acts/C-10.7/FullText.html.

5

Foreign Tax Credits

Living internationally has its challenges! Two or more countries will want to tax you on the same income. As a US citizen or green card holder living in Canada, the US will continue to tax you on your worldwide income, and Canada will also tax you on your worldwide income. As you can see, you are potentially subject to double tax. If everyone wants a piece of your hard-earned money, then how do you avoid paying tax more than once?

Fortunately, there are two solutions to a double-tax scenario. The first option is discussed in Chapter 4, which provides specifics about which country gets to tax what income. The primary goal of the Treaty is to prevent double taxation. The second option to avoid double taxation is through foreign tax credits, which is the topic of this chapter.

You should make note that many retail tax preparation software packages do not handle foreign tax credits properly. Of course, since you are not an expert on foreign tax credits, you have no way of knowing whether your software handles them correctly or not. To make matters worse, there are several other cross-border issues that retail software packages do not handle properly or in some cases, address at all.

We have been preparing complex tax returns for over 25 years, and we are still amazed by the number of people who tell us that they have a simple situation. We have news for you: If you are reading this book, you do not have a simple situation. We recommend that you seek a professional experienced in cross-border taxes. The professional will have the experience, know-how, and resources such as professional tax preparation software to do the job properly.

1. What Are Foreign Tax Credits?

A foreign income tax credit is available to any Canadian who has been a resident of Canada at any time during a tax year. The foreign tax credit directly decreases the income tax payable and works to prevent you from paying tax twice on the same income, particularly if that income is made in a country that has a tax treaty with Canada, like the US. The foreign tax credit is a federal, nonrefundable tax credit; the term "nonrefundable" means the credit is limited by the amount of an individual's tax liability and the credit can only reduce your tax liability to zero. A refundable credit would allow you to take your tax liability below zero and therefore would allow you to receive a refund. Each of the provinces has an equivalent foreign tax credit for income tax paid to a foreign country or countries, and if the federal foreign credit is less than the related tax paid to the foreign country, you may be eligible to claim a provincial foreign tax credit as well as the federal one.

Note: The purpose of the foreign tax credit is to prevent being taxed twice on the same income, therefore you cannot receive a foreign tax credit on income that is not subject to tax in both countries, even if the income is foreign.

2. The Foreign Tax Credit in Canada

The first step to claiming your credit in Canada is to determine the source of foreign income. There are two types of foreign tax credits available: a foreign tax credit for business income taxes and a foreign tax credit for non-business income. Also, the foreign tax credit is calculated on a country-by-country basis that requires taxpayers to categorize their income based on where and how the income was earned.

It is not always easy to determine what constitutes business income. The term "business income" is not exclusively defined in the *Income Tax Act*. This, along with the fact that business income and property income are both derived from activities undertaken in pursuit of profit, makes the determination difficult. One way to make the determination is to analyze the activity undertaken to earn the income. For example, income earned from a passive investment (where income is derived from the ownership of the property rather than the use of the property or the actions of the individual or his or her employees) is characterized generally as property income rather than business income.

Rental income can be especially problematic when trying to decide whether the income is from a business activity or a non-business activity. It is the nature and extent of services provided by a landlord that determine whether the income received by the landlord is considered property income or business income. Generally, income will be considered property income if only basic services are provided to tenants such as heat, light, parking, and laundry facilities. If other services like cleaning, security, and meals are provided, the income is more likely to be considered business income. The more additional services, the more likely it will be considered a business. A good example of this is to compare the services in the rental of an apartment building versus a hotel. A landlord of an apartment building may provide common-area maintenance and not many other direct services, whereas a hotel typically provides many more services like maids, linen, toiletries, laundry, security, and food services. Income from the apartment building is income from property in this example, and income from a hotel is income from a business. If the apartment building landlord provides significantly more services, then income from the apartment building could also be considered business income.

In order for payments to qualify for purposes of a foreign tax credit, the amount paid must be an income tax. Some taxes are not income taxes and do not qualify for tax credits, such as social security tax, sales tax, real estate tax, Value Added Tax (VAT), and customs tax. There is a notable exception to this, however; payments made under the US Federal Insurance Contributions Act, more commonly known as FICA, do qualify as tax for foreign tax credit purposes.

If you contrast the US and Canadian foreign tax credit forms, the calculation of foreign tax credits is much easier in Canada than in the US.

2.1 Foreign non-business income tax credit

If a resident of Canada pays non-business income tax to a government of a country or a state, a deduction against the Canadian tax paid on that income may be claimed. The deduction is limited to the lesser of the non-business income tax paid for the year and the proportion of the Canadian tax for the year related to the foreign-source income. A formula is used to calculate the proportion of Canadian tax paid on the income is as follows:

(Foreign-Source Income)/(Worldwide Income) X
Canadian tax payable

The credit is calculated on a country-by-country basis.

To determine what is included in non-business income tax paid for the purpose of the foreign non-business income tax credit limit, certain foreign taxes are excluded, including:

- Any portion of the foreign tax paid that related to income subject to the overseas employment tax credit. Any portion of taxes paid that would not have been payable if the individual had been a citizen of that country and that cannot reasonably be regarded as being attributable to income from a source outside of Canada (e.g., because the US taxes citizens on world income, a US citizen residing in Canada who pays US tax on Canadian-source income cannot consider this tax as foreign taxes paid).

- Any portion of taxes that are generally deductible elsewhere in the tax return.

- Any portion of taxes that will be refunded by the foreign government.

Before the amount of tax can be used in the calculation of the foreign tax credit, it must be determined to have been paid for the year for which you are liable to pay the tax on income considered to have been earned for that year according to the foreign jurisdiction's laws, even though the income may not be recognized in Canada in the same year. To calculate the credit, the tax paid must be converted into Canadian currency using an appropriate rate of exchange. If the withholding rate or the tax rate paid to the foreign jurisdiction is greater than a rate specified in a treaty between Canada and that country, then the excess is not considered foreign tax paid. Instead, you should seek a refund of the excess from the foreign revenue authorities. The credit is based on the ultimate net tax paid to the foreign country attributable to income from a source outside of Canada (e.g., because the US taxes citizens on world income, a US citizen residing in Canada who pays US tax on Canadian-source income cannot consider this tax as foreign taxes paid).

The tax must have been paid by you, not your spouse, children, corporation, or anyone other than the you. If the tax was paid by a partnership, you percentage share of the tax can be included. If the tax was paid jointly with a spouse (as is usually the case when tax returns are filed jointly in the US), the amount paid can be allocated between you and your spouse, generally in proportion to each spouse's respective foreign income that was the basis for the tax.

In determining what constitutes foreign-source income, the *Income Tax Act* does not provide specific rules for determining the source of an income amount. However, there are guidelines:

- A gain on the disposition of shares is sourced to the location where the sale takes place, and, in the case of stocks and bonds, the location of the stock exchange in which the security is sold.

- A gain on the disposition of real property is sourced to the country where the property is located.

- Interest income is usually based on the residency of the debtor who is paying the interest.

- Dividends are usually based on the residency of the corporation paying the dividends.

- Rental income is usually based on the country where the property is located or used.

- Employment income is based on where employment duties are performed.

- Services are based on the place where services are performed.

- Merchandise trading is based on the place where the sales are habitually completed.

Tax-exempt income is not included in the determination of foreign source income included in the formula. Tax-exempt income is considered to include income that is exempt from tax because of a treaty. CRA wants to ensure that the foreign tax credit does not reduce Canadian tax on any portion of foreign income not subject to foreign tax.

As an example of this, consider a situation where a Canadian citizen owns US corporate bonds that pay interest to her. Article XI of the Treaty provides that there is no withholding tax on interest; therefore, she does not pay tax to the US but does pay tax on the income in Canada. In this example, the interest could not be included in the numerator of the formula as foreign source income. Another similar example is a dual US-Canadian citizen who lives in Canada and owns the same bonds. The interest would be taxable to the dual citizen when he files his US income tax return; therefore, it would be included in the numerator as foreign source income for the dual citizen because he did, in fact, have a tax obligation to the US on the interest income.

For individual taxpayers, the total non-business income foreign tax credit cannot exceed 15% of the foreign source non-business income. So, if you paid taxes to foreign countries, and the total combined tax rate was in excess of 15%, you could end up in a double-tax situation. The *Income Tax Act* provides that if the foreign-source non-business income exceeds 15%, then the excess can be deducted instead. However, a deduction does not provide a direct reduction in the taxes to be paid.

The foreign non-business income tax credit must be used in the year in which the foreign tax was levied. There are several situations that could arise when there is a mismatch of when the foreign country will recognize the income and levy the tax and when Canada will recognize the income. Two common examples of this are installment sales and Section 1031 exchanges in the US.

If property is sold using an installment sale that would be subject to both US and Canadian taxes for an individual, Canada does allow taxpayers to defer a portion of capital gains through a reserve, but the amount that can be deferred is limited to payment over five years. An installment sale in the US is unlimited as to the term. Care would have to be taken in a situation where an installment sale of US property owned by a Canadian taxpayer so that the terms of the installment sale conform to the Canadian five-year payout rules; otherwise, there would be a mismatch of when income would be recognized in the US versus Canada.

The other example is an IRS Code Section 1031 (or "like-kind") exchange of investment property. This provision provides that no gain or loss is recognized in the US when a taxpayer exchanges property solely for like-kind property. This provision allows many US taxpayers to avoid capital gain on the sale of US real (or certain business) property by acquiring similar property, generally with a higher value, within a specified period of time. It allows the US taxpayer to continually trade up his or her property indefinitely without incurring capital gains until the last piece of property is sold. Canada does not recognize this deferral, so for a Canadian taxpayer, capital gain or loss is recognized when each property is sold. Because there is no tax in the US, there is no offsetting foreign source income nor foreign tax credit to offset the capital gain in Canada when each property is sold. Instead, at the time of the sale of the very last property, the US will recognize the net capital gain or loss realized on all of the properties. For the Canadian taxpayer who would try to use the 1031 exchange provisions in the US to defer the tax in the US, he or she would end up having paid double tax on the properties because of the mismatch of the timing of when gain was recognized.

2.2 Foreign business-income tax credit

When an individual carries on a business in a foreign jurisdiction and the business income is subject to an income or profits tax in the other country or jurisdiction, the business foreign tax credit deduction is calculated in much the same way as the non-business income foreign tax credit. However, unlike the non-business income tax credit that has a 15% tax limit, there is no limit on the amount of foreign tax paid that is eligible for the foreign business income tax credit.

Another important difference between the non-business income foreign tax credit and the business income foreign tax credit is that there is a three-year carry back and ten-year carry forward available for foreign taxes paid on business income. This provides for a better matching of when the credit is available to when the income is recognized in both countries.

3. The Foreign Tax Credit in the US

The US foreign tax credit system is more complicated and potentially less efficient than the Canadian system. By less efficient, we mean that you are more likely to have some degree of double tax because the foreign tax credit may not completely offset the foreign tax paid.

Note: If you are a Canadian resident, we generally recommend taking the foreign tax credit on the Canadian return rather than on the US return.

The US has five different income categories. The credit has to be calculated separately for each category, and excess income in one category cannot be used to offset excess credits in another category. For example, you may receive interest payments where little or no tax is due on that income. You may also have a pension that generated a lot of tax that could not be completely offset by the foreign tax credit and a carryover resulted. If you were able to combine the two incomes into one bucket and recalculate the tax, you would have had a larger tax credit, but that is not allowed.

Though there are five categories, you will typically only be concerned with two: Passive and General Limitation. The passive income category includes income such as interest, dividends, capital gains, annuity payments, and rents. The definition of general limitation income is any income that does not fit into one of the other categories, but essentially it boils down to earned income and pensions.

There is no need for us to go into great detail on the US foreign tax credit calculation since we are recommending that in most cases you not use the US, but rather take the foreign tax credit in Canada.

6

Retirement Plans, Pensions, and Social Security

1. US Taxation of Canadian Retirement Plans

1.1 Canadian pension contributions

All Canadian residents living and earning income in Canada are eligible to contribute to Registered Retirement Savings Plans (RRSPs) and other similar, qualified retirement plans. An RRSP is not an investment, such as a stock or bond, but rather it is an investment wrapper similar to a traditional Individual Retirement Account (IRA) or 401(k) in the US. It is a trust under which a trustee holds eligible investments for the beneficiary of the trust (you). The trustees of RRSPs are commercial trustees, such as a trust company or custodian. Contributions to an RRSP are tax deductible on your Canadian return (T1) as long as the deduction meets the current contribution limit which is the lower of 18% of the taxpayer's earned income for two years prior. Additional contributions can be made to catch up on prior years' contributions that were not made up to the prior years' contribution limits ("contribution room"). Contribution room carries forward until it is funded by the taxpayer or until the RRSP matures on December 31 of the year you turn age 71 (see below for more details).

Each year after you file your tax return, CRA will send you a Notice of Assessment. As part of that Notice of Assessment, the CRA will let you know how much contribution room you have available.

Under the Fifth Protocol to the Treaty which came into effect in 2009, a US citizen or green card holder living in Canada who works for a Canadian employer is permitted to deduct the RRSP or other qualified retirement plan contributions on his or her US tax return, just as it would for a generally similar US plan. Thus, a US taxpayer can only deduct RRSP contributions up to the limits allowed for similar US plans. For 2016, the US permits pre-tax deductions for 401(k) plan contributions of up to $18,000 USD. There is no contribution room or catch-up permitted for US taxpayers except for an additional $6,000 USD per year (2016) that can be contributed by individuals who are over the age 50, making the total maximum contribution $24,000 USD per year. The result for a US taxpayer living and working in Canada is that he or she should only contribute up to the lowest annual limit permitted by either country.

1.2 Spousal RRSP

If you are married or in a common-law relationship, you may choose to direct some or all of your RRSP contribution to a spousal plan. You still get the tax deduction, but the plan is registered in your spouse's name. Your contributions to a spousal plan do not affect your spouse's contribution limit to his or her own plan.

If you and your spouse earn different levels of income, a spousal RRSP may be an effective way to split income over the long-term. To do so, the spouse who is expected to have a higher level of income at retirement should make the contribution to a spousal RRSP. This will allow you to build a nest egg that will provide each of you with a source of income in retirement and an overall reduction in taxes. Remember, that in Canada, couples file their own returns and pay tax based only on their income.

Note: Even though couples will be filing separate returns in Canada, they should typically file a joint return in the US.

1.3 Pension withdrawals

All registered retirement plan accounts in Canada mature on December 31 of the year in which the owner turns 71. When the plans mature you have four choices: convert it to a registered retirement income fund (RRIF), use the proceeds to purchase a registered annuity, take a lump-sum, or some combination of the above. A RRIF is an arrangement under which the trustee can pay the annuitant at least a statutorily required minimum distribution amount each year. It is possible to take cash from an RRSP directly before it matures although the funds will be subject to a withholding tax based on the amount withdrawn, which ranges from 10% for amounts up to $5,000 CAD and 30% for amounts over $15,000 CAD. When the RRSP is converted to an RRIF, however, there is no withholding tax requirement on distributions from the RRIF but there is a minimum required distribution, even if an RRSP is transferred to an RRIF before it matures. All distributions are subject to Canadian income tax. The US does not make you change accounts when you reach mandatory distribution age, but Canada does. So think of an RRSP like an IRA in the accumulation phase and an RRIF as the IRA in the mandatory distribution phase.

There are different rules for nonresidents, so if you ever decide to leave Canada (return to the US for example) you will need to follow different rules. We suggest that you read our book *Taxation of Canadians in America* (also published by Self-Counsel Press) if you move to the US.

For US tax purposes, the Treaty allows for the deferral of income in all registered savings plans which include RRSPs and RRIFs. Until a few years ago, the deferral was only permitted when a disclosure form was filed with the IRS; however, that disclosure is no longer required and deferral is automatically granted at the federal level. Because the contributions were deductible for both Canadian and US tax purposes, all distributions received by the US taxpayer must be included in gross income. In other words, when the taxpayer receives distributions from an RRSP, the entire amount of each distribution will be subject to US income tax.

Important: The tax treatment of registered retirement plans for a US citizen or US taxpayer who is living in Canada is very different than for someone who is a Canadian citizen (who is not also a dual US citizen or US taxpayer) who moves to the US. Those persons would be able to defer US tax on income from the RRSPs. However, when money is withdrawn, they would only be taxed on deferred earnings and not be taxed on original contributions to the RRSP. Some of you may have a combination of contributions that were deductible and not deductible in the US; for those of you in this situation, a portion will be taxable and a portion will be tax-free. Consult an experienced cross-border tax adviser to determine how your Canadian registered account will be taxed in the US.

1.4 Old Age Security and Canadian Pension Plan contributions and benefits

Old Age Security (OAS) is a Canadian government program that provides all individuals who meet certain Canadian residency requirements with universal access to a basic level of retirement income. To qualify for a full benefit, you must have resided in Canada for 40 years after reaching age 18. A prorated benefit is available for persons who have lived in Canada for at least ten years after age 18. The maximum current OAS benefit is $570.52 CAD per month (January to March 2016), regardless of your marital status. Benefits begin at age 65, but if a taxpayer's income is over a certain threshold ($73,756.40 CAD for 2016), the Canadian government imposes a special tax (a "clawback") to take back a portion of the OAS benefits paid to higher income taxpayers. For each $1 of income above the limit, the amount of the OAS benefit is reduced by $0.15. Once a taxpayer reaches an income level of $119,398 (2016), the benefit is completely clawed back. In other words, a taxpayer has no benefit from OAS if they make over $119,398 in 2016. Any amounts received and not clawed back are fully taxable in Canada.

The Canadian Pension Plan (CPP) is a federally administered program designed to provide monthly retirement pensions to qualified contributors and their dependents upon their death. Quebec has its own provincially administered plan (Quebec Pension Plan or QPP). CPP contributions are paid by everyone who works in Canada, with a few exceptions. The employer and employee share 50/50 in the contributions, and self-employed persons contribute 100%. The current contribution rates as a percentage of earnings is 4.95% (5.325% in Quebec) up to a maximum contribution of $2,544.30 CAD ($2,737.05 CAD in Quebec), for the year 2016. Contributions by employees result in nonrefundable federal and provincial tax credits on your Canadian T1 return. The maximum CPP retirement benefit for recipients at age 65 is $1,092.50 CAD per month (2016). Benefits can begin as early as age 62 with a reduced monthly benefit or as late as age 70 with an increased monthly benefit. For those retiring in 2016, your monthly benefit is reduced by 0.6% for each month that you receive your pension before age 65. In other words, a pension taken at age 62 will be 21.6% (36 months times 0.6%) less than a pension taken at age 65. Benefits received are fully taxable to the recipient in Canada.

For US income tax purposes, OAS and CPP/QPP are taxed in the same way that US taxpayers report social security income. The benefits are generally not taxable if your income (including the CPP/QPP/OAS) is less than $25,000 USD if you are single, or $32,000 USD for a married couple. If your income is between $25,000 USD and $34,000 USD for singles, and between $32,000 USD and $44,000 USD for couples, 50% of your benefits are taxable; if your income exceeds $34,000 USD for singles ($44,000 USD for a married couple), then only 85% of your benefit is subject to income tax and 15% is tax free. There is no clawback for OAS, so even if you do not receive an actual benefit because your OAS was clawed back, your total OAS income (before clawback) will still be taxable in the US. Think of it as receiving OAS, then being subject to a 100% tax.

2. Canadian Taxation of US Retirement Plans

2.1 Contributions to US retirement accounts

After moving to Canada, you as a US taxpayer should not continue to contribute to your US retirement accounts such as IRAs, 401(k)s, and the like. Canada does not give a similar tax deduction for Canadian taxpayers, working in Canada, who contribute to US retirement accounts.

Important: If you own a US Roth IRA account, you should be especially careful not to make a contribution to the Roth IRA as a Canadian taxpayer. The Fifth Protocol specifically provides that contributions made to a Roth IRA by a Canadian resident taxpayer will eliminate the tax benefits of owning a Roth IRA that are afforded through the Treaty. In the US, contributions to Roth IRAs are not tax deductible, the money grows tax-free, and distributions from it are not taxable. The Fifth Protocol provides that if a US person moves to Canada with a Roth IRA, the Roth IRA earnings would not be taxable in Canada as well. Any income accrued within the IRA and all withdrawals from the IRA will continue to be tax-free in both Canada and the US as long as you follow these rules.

To enjoy the benefit in Canada, you are required to make a one-time irrevocable election for each Roth IRA to defer Canadian tax on income earned in the IRA. The election should be made in the form of a letter for each Roth IRA and, in addition to various administrative information, you should include a statement signed by the account owner indicating that you "elect to defer Canadian taxation under paragraph 7 of Article XVIII of the Canada-US Income Tax Convention with respect to any income accrued in the Roth IRA for all taxation years ending before or after the date of the election, until such time as a Canadian Contribution in made." Each of the letters should be sent to the Canadian Competent Authority Services Division in Ottawa, postmarked no later than the due date of the first year's tax return, to:

International and Large Business Directorate
Competent Authority Services Division
427 Laurier Avenue West
8th Floor, Enterprise Building
Ottawa, Ontario K1A 0L5

Phone: 613-941-2768
Fax: 613-990-7370
Email: MAP-APA.PAA-APP@cra-arc.gc.ca

There is a provision for Canadian taxpayers who are on short-term cross-border assignments or commute daily to work for a US employer to deduct contributions made to a US qualified retirement plan on their Canadian tax returns. Qualified retirement plans in the US include traditional 401(k) plans and other similar plans. Canada will allow a deduction for the contribution to the 401(k) plan, but the deduction is limited to the lower of the amount allowed under US law or the RRSP contribution limit for the year (after taking into account RRSP contributions otherwise deducted).

2.2 Pension withdrawals

CRA provides little guidance as to how US retirement accounts are to be treated when owned by a Canadian taxpayer who is also a US citizen or green card holder. Fortunately, the Treaty provides specific guidance.

For Canadian tax purposes, the Treaty allows for the deferral of income in all qualified retirement plans which include most common tax-sheltered retirement plans such as 401(k) plans and IRAs.

When withdrawals are taken from the US retirement plan accounts, they will be taxed in both Canada and the US similarly. A distribution from a traditional deductible IRA or 401(k) will be fully taxed to you in the US at your ordinary income tax rates. It will also become part of your taxable income in Canada. You will be able to use a foreign tax credit to offset the taxes paid to the US. If you have an after-tax Roth IRA account, you will be able to reduce your taxable benefit by the amount you contributed for both US and Canadian tax purposes. Note that if you take an early withdrawal from a US qualified plan account (generally a withdrawal before the age of 59), a 10% early withdrawal tax will be applied in the US. Because this is a penalty, it is not eligible for the foreign tax credit.

If you are a member of a defined benefit plan or a deferred compensation plan in the US that is or was offered through your employer, these benefits, when paid, will be included in your taxable income in Canada most of the time. If the employer made all of the contributions on your behalf, then the full amount will be taxable to you when received. If you made all of the contributions, then CRA concluded that the benefit is not treated as a retirement account, instead it is determined to be a capital investment account. Thus, distributions will be treated as only partially taxable — the taxable distributions can be reduced by the amounts you contributed, and the remainder will likely be a capital gain.

2.3 Social security

As a Canadian tax resident, you will still be entitled to receive US Social Security benefits as long as you qualify for the benefits. To qualify for benefits, you or your spouse will have needed to work in the US for at least ten years. The amount of benefit that you will receive is based on the earnings that you or your spouse reported and how much you paid into the Social Security system.

The benefit that you receive will be taxable to you in both Canada and the US. The US typically considers 15% of the amount received as nontaxable, and according to the treaty, a Canadian taxpayer who receives US social security benefits will be taxed on only 85% of the total received. There is no tax relief in Canada for the same income threshold in the US that, as discussed earlier in this chapter, applies to reduce the income tax to zero if the taxpayer's income falls below the threshold. In other words, if an individual dual-citizen Canadian resident's total taxable income is less than $25,000 USD, he or she would not be taxed on any US social security benefit received for US income tax purposes but would still be taxed on 85% of the Social Security benefits in Canada.

2.4 Planning for US retirement accounts

For US citizens or green card holders living in Canada who hold US retirement accounts, there are three options:

- continue to hold the accounts,
- withdraw the money and close out the accounts, or
- transfer the accounts to Canadian RRSPs.

If you choose to continue to hold the accounts, you will be permitted the same benefits and treatment as if the accounts were generally held as RRSP accounts. As long as the plan generally corresponds to a pension or retirement plan established in or recognized for taxpayers in Canada, it will be treated in Canada the same as the Canadian plan. Thus, US traditional IRAs, 401(k)s and other tax-deferred accounts, are considered to be taxable in Canada in the same manner that RRSPs are taxed. This, however, may cause a problem for you in determining when to take required minimum distributions because you will be facing two sets of rules with the same account. The required minimum distribution for US purposes is, for most taxpayers, as shown in Table 8.

For US purposes, the first required minimum distribution payment must be made by April 1 of the year following the year in which you turn 70½ and then by December 31 for every subsequent year. So for the year that you are 71, you would have to take a required minimum distribution calculated by using the required distribution percentage for age 71 from this table by December 31 of the year in which you turned 71. The distribution period is determined by using the age on your birthday during the year. The penalty for failing to take out at least the required minimum distribution is a 50% penalty on the shortfall.

Similarly, the table for determining minimum RRIF distributions is as shown in Table 9.

For Canadian tax purposes, the minimum distributions must begin in the year you turn 71 and are based on the fair market value of the account at the beginning of the year multiplied by percentage from the chart for age 70 (your age at the beginning of the year).

You will have to be careful to take the higher of the two tables and also take into account the foreign exchange conversion so that you don't run afoul of either country's minimum distribution requirements.

> Jill is a dual US-Canadian citizen living in Canada and has turned age 71 in October of this year. She owns an IRA account that was worth $122,000 USD on December 31 of last year. The US-Canada foreign exchange was 1.3000 as of

December 31 of last year. Jill needs to determine her required minimum distribution.

US required distribution calculation (to be paid by April 1 of the following year because she turned 70½ this year):

$122,000 x 3.65% (the factor for age 70) = $4,453 USD

Canadian required distribution calculation (to be paid by December 31 of the current year):

$122,000 x 1.3000 x 5.0% = $7,930 CAD (or $6,100 USD)

Jill should take a distribution from her IRA before December 31 of the current year for $6,100 USD to comply with both the Canadian and US rules for making a required minimum distribution from her IRA account this year.

Table 8
US REQUIRED MINIMUM DISTRIBUTION TABLE
(TABLE III UNIFORM LIFETIME TABLE*)

Age at December 31	Required Distribution Expressed as a % of the Account	Age at December 31	Required Distribution Expressed as a % of the Account
70	3.65%	86	7.09%
71	3.77%	87	7.46%
72	3.91%	88	7.87%
73	4.05%	89	8.33%
74	4.20%	90	8.77%
75	4.37%	91	9.26%
76	4.55%	92	9.80%
77	4.72%	93	10.42%
78	4.93%	94	10.99%
79	5.13%	95	11.63%
80	5.35%	96	12.35%
81	5.59%	97	13.16%
82	5.85%	98	14.08%
83	6.13%	99	14.93%
84	6.45%	100	15.87%
85	6.76%	101	16.95%

*for most US taxpayers, unless the spouse is the sole beneficiary of the account and is more than ten years younger than you.

Table 9
MINIMUM RRIF DISTRIBUTIONS (CANADA)

Age at December 31	Required Distribution Expressed as a % of the Account	Age at December 31	Required Distribution Expressed as a % of the Account
70	5.00%	86	8.99%
71	5.28%	87	9.55%
72	5.40%	88	10.21%
73	5.53%	89	10.99%
74	5.67%	90	11.92%
75	5.82%	91	13.06%
76	5.98%	92	14.49%
77	6.17%	93	16.34%
78	6.36%	94	18.79%
79	6.58%	95	20.00%
80	6.82%	96	20.00%
81	7.08%	97	20.00 %
82	7.38%	98	20.00 %
83	7.71%	99	20.00 %
84	8.08%	100	20.00 %
85	8.51%	101	20.00 %

Your next option is to withdraw the amounts in your US retirement accounts. If you do, you should be aware of the taxes you will face, especially if you have not reached age 71. In the US, the withdrawal will be taxed at your ordinary income tax rates, and if you are not yet 59, you will also be taxed an additional 10% as an early withdrawal tax. The withdrawal also will be fully taxable to you in Canada as taxable income. You will be able to use the taxes that you pay to the US, including the early withdrawal tax (because it is classified as a tax and not a penalty), as foreign tax credits to offset your Canadian tax that will be due from the withdrawal.

2.5 Rolling your US account into an RRSP

The Canadian *Income Tax Act* allows the transfer of amounts from an IRA or a 401(k) to an RRSP on a tax-deferred basis. However, this is problematic because, while Canada allows a tax-free transfer, the US does not. The US will tax the withdrawal at your marginal tax rate for a US citizen or green card holder (plus an additional 10% early withdrawal penalty if the owner is under age 59). This may put you in a double-tax situation because you will pay tax to the US in the year of the transfer, but you won't pay tax to Canada until the year of withdrawal. Unless you have another source of foreign income to apply the credits to in the year of transfer, you may lose those credits.

Table 10
PROS AND CONS OF ROLLING 401(K) OR IRA TO AN RRSP

PROS	CONS
Simplify your financial situation	Pay tax early and FTC may not be available
Able to manage your investments yourself	10% penalty if under 59 ½ years of age
	Higher investment costs in Canada
	Fewer investment choices in Canada

3. The Totalization Agreement and the Windfall Elimination Provision (WEP)

Canada and the US entered into an agreement with regard to social security benefits. As an American living in Canada, you should be aware of this agreement, especially if you have not accumulated sufficient time in Canada to be eligible for Canadian Old Age Security. The agreement provides that for purposes of determining the time requirement for OAS, Canada should consider a quarter of coverage credited under the US laws as three months of residence in Canada. What this means is that the combined time spent in both the US and Canada can be used to determine whether or not you have met the time requirement for obtaining OAS which, as discussed earlier in this chapter, is 40 years after the age of 18 for a full benefit or a prorated benefit for being resident at least 10 years after age 18.

You may also qualify for benefits from both Canada and the US according to the agreement. After determining eligibility, each country will pay a benefit based solely on your periods of contribution or periods of residence under its pension program.

While this is not a tax issue, it is often an area of concern and confusion. You may find that Social Security Administration employees are often not aware of the agreement and follow the basic rules provided by the Social Security Administration with regard to benefits from more than one country through the Windfall Elimination Provision (WEP). WEP may apply whenever you worked in a job where you earned foreign social security benefits (like CPP or QPP) without paying US Social Security taxes. If it is determined that the WEP applies to you, your US Social Security benefits can be reduced by as much as 60%. If the Social Security Administration tells you that you are subject to WEP, we suggest that you read the US-Canada Agreement on Social Security carefully and appeal your case. See the Resources at the back of this book for where to find this text.

The WEP was intended to prevent federal workers and certain union workers from qualifying for Social Security benefits when they had not paid into Social Security. We believe that both governments are incorrectly applying the WEP and inappropriately reducing benefits in many cases. We cannot help you with your WEP matter, but if you are interested in appealing your case, we might be able to refer you to an attorney willing to accept your case.

7

Investing in Canada

In a lot of ways, investing in Canada is similar to investing in the US, however there are also significant differences. Because this is a book about taxes we will not go into great detail, but we will outline the Canadian investment landscape and how different types of investment income and products are taxed. We will talk in more detail about some types of investment options that you may want to avoid because of the US tax headaches.

1. Comparing the US and Canadian Securities Markets

The Canadian market is much smaller than the US market, and maybe more importantly the financial services industry is dominated by Canada's five big banks: Royal Bank of Canada (RBC), Toronto Dominion Bank (TD Canada Trust), Bank of Nova Scotia (Scotiabank), Bank of Montreal (BMO), and Canadian Imperial Bank of Commerce (CIBC). Because of the smaller market and lack of competition, the costs associated with investing in Canada are significantly higher than the costs in the US. In fact, the internal management fees of Canadian mutual funds are the highest in the world according to "Canadian Securities Administrators Discussion Paper and Request for Comment 81-407," (December, 2012: https://www.osc.gov.on.ca/documents/en/Securities-Category8/csa_2012123_81-407_rfc-mutual-fund-fees.pdf).

The Canadian stock market, as denoted by the Toronto Stock Exchange (TSX), is approximately one tenth the size of the US stock market, as denoted by the Standard and Poors Total Market Index as can be seen in Table 11 (data as of close-of-market December 31, 2014).

Table 11
STOCK MARKETS

	S&P/TSX Composite (Canada)	S&P Total Market Index (US)
Number of Companies Listed	250	3,920
Adjusted Market Cap. ($ Billions)	$2,090 CAD	$24,655 USD
Top 10 Holdings (as a % Market Cap)	36.1%	14.1%

Because market capitalization in the TSX drops off sharply, the market is more concentrated in a relatively small number of stocks, as can be seen in differences in the Top 10 Holdings Market Share.

The Canadian stock market is far less diversified than the US stock market, and is highly dependent on just three sectors; financials; energy; and materials (gold and mining) which together make up over 68% of the Canadian market. Therefore, if you purchase only Canadian securities you will not have sufficient sector diversification. Table 12 gives a comparison across all of the Global Industry Classification Standard (GIC) sectors.

Table 12
STOCK SECTORS

GICS® Sector	S&P/TSX Composite (Canada)	S&P Total Market Index (US)
Financials	35.7	18.0
Energy	22.0	7.6
Materials	10.6	3.6
Industrials	8.7	11.3
Consumer Discretionary	6.4	12.9
Telecommunication Services	4.9	2.0
Consumer Staples	3.7	8.5
Health Care	3.5	14.0
Information Technology	2.3	19.0
Utilities	2.2	3.3

According to the Canadian Securities Administrators paper on mutual fund fees, important differences include:

- Canadian stock market returns have generally been lower than the US, but bond returns have been higher.

- Canadian tax laws do not distinguish between short-term and long-term capital gains. In the US you must hold a security for at least one year and a day to qualify for the preferred long-term capital gains tax treatment. All capital gains in Canada are taxed on one-half of the gain. The other way of looking at it is that the capital gains tax rate is one-half of the marginal tax rate.

- Unlike the US tax system, one cannot designate which lot(s) of shares are to be sold when placing a sell order, and cannot choose between first-in-first-out, average cost, or specific lots. In Canada, the adjusted cost base per share (i.e., average cost) is used to determine the gain or loss.

- The dividend tax credit in Canada makes dividend investing in a taxable account more attractive than it is in the US. Corporate income is taxed twice in the US, once at the corporate level and once again in the hands of the shareholders when a dividend is paid. Whereas in Canada, the individual receives a tax credit for certain dividends received. The concept is to give you credit for the taxes already paid by the corporation.

- Canada does not allow tax-free treatment of municipal bonds.

- Canada does not allow tax-deferred treatment of annuities or cash value life insurance.

- In the US you can easily buy Treasury bonds at auction using the Treasury Direct website whereas in Canada you have to buy them on the secondary market, which means that you are paying a bid ask spread to the broker.

- There are also some terminology differences. For example, a US Certificate of Deposit (CD) is similar to a Canadian Guaranteed Investment Certificate (GIC), and US Treasury Inflation Protected Securities (TIPS) are similar to Real Return Bonds (RRBs). Canadian RRBs, unlike US TIPS, do not have a $100 face value minimum, so, if there is extended deflation the RRBs could be worth less than the issue price.

- Deposit Insurance limits are different as well. In the US, Federal Deposit Insurance Corporation (FDIC) protection is for $250,000 USD per account whereas for Canadians, the Canadian Deposit Insurance Corporation (CDIC) protection limit is $100,000 CAD per account.

- For Canadian investors in taxable accounts, you make the transaction on the settlement date and in the US you make the transaction on the trade date. The settlement date is the date which a buyer must pay for the securities delivered by the seller and the trade is the date when the order to purchase, sell or otherwise acquire a security is performed.

Table 13
A US-CANADA STOCK MARKET COMPARISON

Typical Management Fees (MER)	Median	Asset-Weighted Average
Money Market	1.00	0.89
Fixed Income	1.50	1.38
Balanced	1.95	1.82
Equity	2.00	1.91

Comparison of US versus Canada Description	Canada	United States
Total Mutual Fund Assets	762,000,000	12,814,200,000
Number of Fund Providers	103	713
Share of funds held by top 10% of providers	75%	53%
Number of Mutual Funds	2,667	7,637
Average Fund Size	242,000,000	1,580,000,000
Asset-weighted Ave. MER	1.93%	0.79%

To get the total cost of running a Canadian mutual fund, you have to add the Trading Expense Ratio, whereas the US expresses its fund expenses as Total Expenses Ratios, with the trading expenses included. The average trading expense ratio for Canadian mutual funds was 0.14% in 2011.

We believe that how Canadian investment services are delivered is ten years (or more) behind the US and here is why we think so:

- The vast majority (69%) of services continue to be delivered in a sales format with commissioned salespeople, so beware that regardless how nice these people may seem, they are not required to look out for your best interests.

- Until July of 2016, neither the financial institutions nor the advisors were required to provide performance data or investment fees.

- Automatic downloads from the custodians to the advisor's investment software is nonexistent, whereas in the US every advisor is allowed free daily downloads.

- Canadian wrap fees, or fees based on assets under management, average about 2 to 2.5%, whereas the average fee in the US is 1 to 1.2%.

- Only recently were Exchange Traded Funds (ETFs) available in Canada and it continues to be difficult to find a sufficient number of ETFs to complete a well-diversified portfolio.

- The Canadian securities regulation is not overseen by one national organization like it is in the US, so rules and requirements can vary between provinces.

- In general, financial advisors in Canada are not required to follow a fiduciary standard; meaning they do not have to look out for your best interests, unlike advisors registered with the US Securities and Exchange Commission (SEC). All SEC registered advisors are required to place their clients' interests ahead of their own.

2. Taxation of Dividends in Canada

There are three types of dividends you can receive from your corporation: an eligible dividend, a regular dividend (also referred to as an ineligible dividend), or a capital dividend (capital dividends are received tax-free).

2.1 Eligible dividend rules

These rules apply to certain dividends paid by corporations resident in Canada to shareholders resident in Canada. For 2016, dividends designated as eligible dividends are subject to a dividend gross-up of 38% and a federal dividend tax credit equal to 20.73% of the actual dividend.

Taxable dividends from Canadian resident corporations that are not designated as eligible dividends are ineligible (or regular) dividends. For 2016, these dividends are subject to a 17% dividend gross-up. The 2015 federal budget has proposed to reduce both the dividend gross-up and the federal dividend tax credit for regular dividends over a four-year period, beginning in 2016. This will result in a gradual increase in the tax rate applicable to regular dividends to coincide with the decline in the corporate small-business rate. This is intended to maintain integration of the tax system. The provinces all have their own dividend tax credit rates (refer to the individual tax tables for a comparison of the top marginal eligible and ineligible dividend rates by province).

As a result of the dividend gross-up and tax credit mechanism, dividends are taxed more favorably than most other types of income (except for capital gains).

Dividends received from a foreign corporation are not subject to the gross-up and dividend tax credit mechanisms. Therefore, you'll pay a higher rate of tax on dividends from a foreign corporation.

2.2 Dividends and corporations

A corporation's ability to pay an eligible dividend depends on its status. A Canadian-Controlled Private Corporation (CCPC) can only pay an eligible dividend to the extent that it has a balance in its "general rate income pool" (GRIP) at the end of the taxation year in which the dividend is paid. Although the actual formula is quite complex, the GRIP generally reflects taxable income that has not benefited from preferential tax rates, such as the small business rate, or from refundable dividend tax treatment afforded to investment income earned by a CCPC. There is an exception for public company dividends that have been designated as eligible dividends. Such dividends retain their status as eligible dividends when they pass through a private corporation.

A non-CCPC that is resident in Canada can generally pay eligible dividends without restriction.

2.3 Designating an eligible dividend

For a dividend to be an eligible dividend, it must be designated as such in writing by the corporation paying the dividend. For private corporations, the CRA has indicated that proper notice will include: (i) a letter to the shareholders; (ii) a notation on dividend check stubs; or (iii) in cases where all shareholders are directors, a notation in the corporate minutes. The notification procedure for public corporations is more simplified. Before or at the time the dividend is paid, the corporation only needs to make a designation stating that all dividends are eligible dividends unless indicated otherwise. This designation can generally be found on the corporation's website (under Investor Services). The corporation must make the designation no later than three years following the day on which the dividend was paid.

If a corporation makes an eligible dividend designation that exceeds its capacity, the corporation will be subject to a penalty tax. However, there are special rules that may allow the corporation to retroactively undo all or part of an excessive designation by making an election to treat the excess eligible dividend as being a taxable dividend.

If you are the owner-manager of a CCPC and you want to pay a dividend from the company, consult with your tax advisor to determine if all or part of the dividend should be designated as an eligible dividend.

If you have no other sources of income, you can receive a significant amount of Canadian dividend income and pay little or no tax. The amount will vary depending on your province of residence at the end of the year and whether the dividend is an eligible or an ineligible dividend.

Alternative minimum tax may apply on the receipt of eligible dividends, resulting in a higher than expected tax. The amount the eligible dividend is grossed up is an adjustment of AMT purposes.

3. Basics of the US Net Investment Income Tax (NIIT)

The US Net Investment Income Tax (NIIT) applies at a rate of 3.8% to certain net investment income of individuals, estates, and trusts that have income above the statutory threshold amounts. If owed, the tax is in addition to whatever regular tax is owed. This effectively brings the highest marginal tax rate up to 43.4% for net investment income.

Individuals will owe the tax if they have 1) net investment income, and 2) modified adjusted gross income over the thresholds shown in Table 14.

If you are an individual who is exempt from Medicare taxes, you still may be subject to the NIIT if you have net investment income and also have modified adjusted gross income over the applicable thresholds.

For the NIIT, modified adjusted gross income is adjusted gross income increased by the amount of foreign earned income excluded from gross income. If you have income from Controlled Foreign Corporations (CFCs) or Passive Foreign Investment Companies (PFICs), there may be additional adjustments to your AGI.

Nonresident Aliens (NRAs) are not subject to the Net Investment Income Tax, but as a US citizen or green card holder, you are. If you are married to an NRA, you can make the election under section 6013(g) or 6013(h) to have your spouse treated as a resident alien for purposes of filing as Married Filing Jointly, because there are special rules for a spouse who is considered a resident solely due to the election.

Table 14
THRESHOLDS FOR US NIIT

Filing Status	Threshold Amount*
Married filing jointly	$250,000
Married filing separately	$125,000
Single	$200,000
Head of household (with qualifying person)	$200,000
Qualifying widow(er) with dependent child	$250,000

These threshold amounts are not indexed for inflation, so more people will be subject to this tax in the future.

3.1 Planning opportunities

There is little tax planning that can be done for a Canadian with regards to the NIIT. In the US you would be able to invest in tax-free or tax deferred investments to help reduce the NIIT, but Canada does not offer tax-free or tax deferred investments. A potential planning opportunity is to have the assets that produce Net Investment Income in the NRA spouse's name to avoid the NIIT.

If you are considered a dual-resident individual, but you determine that you are a resident of Canada using the tie-breaker rules of the Treaty and you claim to be a nonresident of the US, you are considered an NRA for purposes of the NIIT.

If you are a dual-status resident of the US for part of the year and an NRA for the other part of the year, you are subject to the NIIT only on the income in the portion of the year during which you were a US resident. The threshold amount is not reduced or prorated for a dual-status resident.

3.2 Net investment income defined

In general, investment income includes, but is not limited to interest, dividends, capital gains, rental and royalty income, non-qualified annuities, income from businesses involved in trading of financial instruments or commodities, and businesses that are passive activities to the taxpayer. Your gross investment income is reduced by expenses that are properly allocable to the income.

Wages; unemployment compensation; operating income from a non-passive business; Social Security Benefits; alimony; tax-exempt interest; self-employment income; Alaska Permanent Fund Dividends; and distributions from certain Qualified Plans are examples of income that is not included in calculating net investment income.

To the extent that gains are not otherwise offset by capital losses, the following gains are common examples of items taken into account in computing net investment income:

1. Gains from the sale of stocks, bonds, and mutual funds.

2. Capital gain distributions from mutual funds.

3. Gains from the sale of investment real estate (including gains from the sale of a second home that is not a primary residence).

4. Gains from the sale of interests in partnerships and S corporations (to the extent the partner or shareholder was a passive owner).

The Net Investment Income Tax does not apply to any amount of gain that is excluded from gross income for regular income tax purposes, but any gain above the excluded amount is included in Net Investment Income.

Examples of deductions that may be properly allocable to Gross Investment Income, include investment interest expense, investment advisory and brokerage fees, expenses related to rental and royalty income, tax preparation fees, fiduciary expenses (in the case of an estate or trust), and state and local income taxes.

3.3 Reporting net investment income

Individuals, estates, and trusts will use Form 8960 and to compute their Net Investment Income Tax. For individuals, the tax will be reported on, and paid with Form 1040. For estates and trusts, the tax will be reported on and paid with Form 1041.

3.4 Foreign tax credits

Foreign income tax credits may not be used to reduce your NIIT liability. However, if you take foreign income taxes as an income tax deduction (versus a tax credit), some (or all) of the deduction amount may be deducted against your NIIT.

Note: A potential planning opportunity is to calculate your tax return taking the foreign tax as a credit and as a deduction to see which is best in your situation.

3.5 Calculation examples

A person filing as a single person has wages of $110,000 and $40,000 of dividends and capital gains. Taxpayer's modified adjusted gross income is $150,000, which is less than the $200,000 statutory threshold, therefore the taxpayer is not subject to the Net Investment Income Tax. The NIIT would apply regardless of where the investment income was earned.

A couple filing a married filing jointly return, has $175,000 of wages. The couple also received $90,000 from a passive partnership interest, which is considered Net Investment Income. The couple's modified adjusted gross income is $265,000. The couple's modified adjusted gross income exceeds the threshold of $250,000 by $15,000. Taxpayer's Net Investment Income is $90,000.

The Net Investment Income Tax is based on the lesser of $15,000 (the amount the couple's modified adjusted gross income exceeds the $250,000 threshold) or $90,000 (Taxpayer's Net Investment Income). The couple owes NIIT of $570 ($15,000 x 3.8%).

4. Savings Accounts for Retirement and Education

4.1 General information

Canada does not have 401(k) or Roth IRA plans. The closest similar plans are the Registered Retirement Savings Plan (RRSP) or the Individual Pension Plan (IPP) and Tax-Free Savings Account (TFSA), respectively. An IPP is a one-person Defined Benefit Pension Plan.

Registered Education Savings Plan (RESP) and the Canadian Education Savings Grant (CESP) are much more generous than most US College Savings Plans (529 Plans), which do not offer government grants. An RESP is a contract between an individual and the provider. Under the contract, the individual names one or more beneficiaries and agrees to make contributions for them, and the provider agrees to pay educational assistance payments (EAPs) to the beneficiaries.

- There is no deduction for an RESP contribution, but the money grows tax-free.

- There are no restrictions on who can be the original contributor under an RESP.

- There are no annual limits for contributions to an RESP, but there is a lifetime contribution limit of $50,000 for each beneficiary.

The account has a maximum contribution term of 32 years and must be completed by the end of the year that includes the 35th anniversary of the opening of the plan, unless it is a specified plan.

Funds can be withdrawn to pay for postsecondary education. Accumulated income and government grants (see below) are then taxed in the hands of the beneficiary. As most children have low incomes, withdrawals are likely to be taxed lightly if at all. Any contributed principal can be withdrawn tax-free by the original contributor.

If the beneficiary does not continue with an education beyond high school, government grants must be repaid and principal returned to the contributor. Accumulated income is taxable (at a penalty rate) in the contributor's hands, although tax may be deferred by contributing the funds to an RRSP.

4.2 Canadian Education Savings Grant (CESG)

Human Resources and Skills Development Canada (HRSDC) provides an incentive for parents, family, and friends to save for a child's postsecondary education by paying a grant based on the amount contributed to an RESP for the child. The CESG money will be deposited directly into the child's RESP.

- The federal government will deposit a Canada Education Savings Grant when contributions are made for children up to age 17.

- Only the first $2,500 of a contribution will be matched in any one year, typically at 20% with some increment for lower income families.

- The lifetime maximum CESG is $7,200 per child.

- Unused CESG room can be carried forward.

5. Real Estate

Canada does not have a principal residence mortgage-interest deduction. Mortgage interest expenses on other personal-use real estate is deductible as investment expenses.

Both sales (GST/PST/HST) and transfer taxes are levied when buying real estate in Canada. A transfer tax is payable in all provinces on any acquisition of real property, except for Alberta and Saskatchewan. These provinces levy a registration/transfer fee on the transfer of real property.

Alberta charges a title registration fee and a mortgage registration fee. The title registration fee is $50, plus $1 for every $5,000 of FMV of the property (.02%). In addition, Alberta charges $50, plus $1 for every $5,000 of the mortgage loan.

Saskatchewan charges a land title fee that is $0 for the first $500 of the purchase price, $25 on the next $7,900 of the purchase price, and 0.3% of the purchase price above $8,400.

In British Columbia, the general rate is 1% on the first $200,000 of the fair market value of the property and 2% on the balance of the fair market value of the property. First-time home buyers are eligible to receive a refund on homes purchased for less than $475,000.

In Manitoba, the general rate is 0% on the first $30,000 on the fair market value of the property, 0.5% on the next $60,000, 1% on the next $60,000, 1.5% on the next $60,000, and 2% on the fair market value of property that exceeds $210,000.

In Nova Scotia, the land transfer tax, payable on the sale price depends on the municipality in which the property is located. The applicable rate ranges from 0% to 1.5%, the latter being the maximum allowed by law. Homes in the Halifax area have a transfer tax of 1.5%.

In New Brunswick, the land transfer tax payable is 0.5% of the assessed value of the property.

In the Northwest Territories there is a transfer tax and a mortgage registration fee. The transfer tax is $1.50 on every $1,000 of property value (.15%), subject to a minimum fee of $100, and $1.00 on every $1,000 of

Table 15
COMPARISON OF 529 PLANS VERSUS RESP ACCOUNTS

Feature	529 Plans	RESPs
Variety of plans	Yes, many state plans; each different	No
Tax deductible contributions	No, but some plans allow for a credit at the state level	No
Tax deferred	Yes	Yes
Annual contribution limits	$14,000 ($28,000 if married filing jointly). Can make a lump-sum contribution that covers five years ($70,000/$140,000). Amounts in excess of this limit is subject to gift taxes.	None as of 2016
Maximum contribution	Varies by state ($235,000 to $475,000)	$50,000
Taxability of withdrawals	No tax if used for "qualified education expenses"	Yes, to the beneficiary
Limitations on who can contribute	No	No

property value greater than $1,000,000. There is also a mortgage fee of $1.00 for every $5,000 of mortgage amount.

In Newfoundland and Labrador, there is a transfer tax or a mortgage registration fee. For properties or mortgages under $500, a flat fee of $100 is charged. For properties exceeding $500, a flat fee of $100 is charged, plus $0.40 for every hundred dollars over $500.

The transfer tax in Yukon is $6 on the first $1,000 of property value, $7.50 on the next $2,000 of property value, $10.50 on the next $2,000 of property value, $1.50 on each $1,000 (or fraction of $1,000) between $5,000 and $10,000 of property value, $0.75 on each $1,000 (or fraction of $1,000) between $10,000 and $25,000 of property value, and $0.25 on each $1,000 (or fraction of $1,000) for property over $25,000.

In Ontario, the general rate is 0.5% on the first $55,000 on the value of consideration of the property, and 1% on the value of consideration that exceeds $55,000 without exceeding $250,000. 1.5% is payable on the value of consideration that exceeds $250,000, without exceed $400,000. If the value of the consideration exceeds $400,000, the tax is 2% and applies to the value of the consideration that exceeds $400,000. There is a rebate available for first-time home buyers, up to a maximum of $2,000. The City of Toronto levies an additional land transfer tax of 0.5% on the first $55,000, an additional 1% on the next $345,000, and an additional 2% on amounts over $400,000. Toronto also allows first-time home buyers an exemption of up to $3,725. Example, for a home in Toronto that was bought for more than $400,000, the transfer tax is 4%.

In Prince Edward Island, the tax is computed at the rate of 1% of the greater of the consideration for the transfer and the assessed value of the real property. There is no transfer tax on property less than $30,000. First-time home buyers are exempt from payment of the real property transfer tax if the purchase price is less than $200,000.

In Quebec, the rate is 0.5% on the first $50,000, 1% on the next $200,000, and 1.5% on the in excess of $250,000. If the transferred property is located in the City of Montreal, an additional tax of 0.5% (i.e., 2% total) is payable on that portion of the amount that exceeds $500,000.

Note: Factor in the cost of the land transfer tax and sales tax (PST/GST/HST) when buying a property in Canada. While buying an existing home does not have sales tax applied, sales tax is applied to the realtor's commission and imposed on new home construction.

5.1 Depreciating real estate

Capital Cost Allowance (CCA) is the means by which property is depreciated in Canada. CCA uses a declining balance method versus the straight line method in the US. In Canada, depreciation is optional, whereas in the US it is required. Because depreciation reduces your adjusted cost basis, you will have a smaller cost basis in the US than in Canada if depreciation is not taken in Canada. This means that the gain will be larger in the US than in Canada. The problem is that whenever the income is not the same, or very close, there is possibility of double tax. If depreciation is not taken in Canada, each year there will be more income on the Canadian return than the US and eventually, when the asset is sold, there will be more income in the US than in Canada. This plays havoc with the foreign tax credits and will typically cause double tax.

8

Common Deductions on Canadian Income Taxes

If you are a US person moving to Canada who has never had any exposure to the Canadian tax system, you are in for a shock. Many tax deductions that you have enjoyed in the US are not going to be available to you as a Canadian taxpayer. When there are deductions or credits available, those deductions and credits are generally very limited in comparison to deductions and credits available in the US. For example, personal mortgage interest, real estate taxes, and state (provincial) taxes are not deductible in Canada. Canada does, however, provide an unlimited capital gain exemption for personal residences while the US only provides a $250,000 USD capital gain exemption (or $500,000 USD per couple) for a personal residence. You will find many similarities, but when you scan a tax return, you will find that the deductible amounts or credits available are usually less than what would be available in the US.

Canadian individual taxes are ordered in a particular way to determine Net Income for Tax Purposes. The components that comprise Net Income for Tax Purposes include net employment income or loss, net business income or loss, capital gains and losses, other sources of income, and other deductions. There are certain deductions that can apply to each of these components, which will be discussed here. Once Net Income for Tax Purposes is determined, additional deductions can be taken to determine taxable income. Once taxable income is determined, the tax is calculated. From that, there are credits available that will also be discussed here, to reduce the tax payable.

Table 16
DETERMINING TAXABLE INCOME IN CANADA:
FEDERAL INDIVIDUAL TAX CALCULATION

	Worldwide income from employment, business, property, and all other non-capital sources (only positive amounts are added here)
Plus	Net capital gains (capital gains minus capital losses)
Minus	Deductions
Minus	Losses from employment, business, property (capital losses), and business investment losses
Equals	Net Income for Tax Purposes
Minus	Division C (Other) Deductions
Equals	Taxable Income
Times	Progressive Tax Rates
Equals	Federal Tax before Credits
Minus	Non-Refundable and Refundable Tax Credits
Equals	Federal Tax Payable

1. Employment or Office Deductions

There are certain expenses that can only be applied against employment income, and generally cannot be used against other sources of income. These expenses are specifically allowed under the *Income Tax Act*. There are restrictions on what types of employees can deduct certain items; whether the person is paid by salary or paid through commissions, or by selling property or negotiating contracts on behalf of an employer. A broad principle underlying employee deductions is the separation of the employee's personal or living expenses from expenses incurred in earning employment income. In order for employment expenses to be allowable, they must be reasonable under the circumstances and will only be allowed if the employee has not been reimbursed for the expenses. Employment income deductions include:

- A pension adjustment for all pensions or levels of retirement savings accrued in a year by or on behalf of the individual in his or her employer's registered pension plan and deferred profit-sharing plan.

- A Registered Pension Plan (RPP) deduction for contributions by an employer or an employee to provide a pension to the employee upon retirement.

- Union, professional, or like dues. This includes professional dues paid to organizations of lawyers, doctors, chartered accountants, and others. Members of trade unions can also deduct annual dues to maintain membership in the union.

- Sales expenses paid by a commissioned employee. Commissioned employees are able to deduct a broader range of expenses than other employees; however, the deductions for sales expenses are limited to the amount of commission or similar amount received during the year. The expenses must be incurred to earn commission employment; must be reasonable; the employee must be required to carry on his or her duties away from the office or the employer's location; the individual must be required to pay for his or her own expenses under the employment contract; and the individual must not receive a nontaxable allowance for travel expenses. It cannot be an expense for recreational facilities or club dues, and the expense cannot be a capital outlay or loss.

- Travel and lodging expenses when the employee is ordinarily required to carry on duties of employment away from the office or the place of business; the employee is required to pay his or own travel expenses; and the expenses are directly a result of carrying on business for the employer.

- Motor vehicle travel expenses can also be deducted with the same conditions given for travel and lodging expenses. Employees can deduct fuel costs; maintenance costs including car washes, oil, grease, and servicing charges; repair costs, licenses, insurance, and eligible leasing costs. Capital cost allowance can be deducted for automobile and aircraft expenses, but with specific restrictions. There can be no deduction for the cost of an automobile in excess of $30,000 CAD and deductible interest is limited to $300 CAD per month (deductible lease payments are limited to $800 CAD per month).

- Home office expenses can be deducted if the employee performs his or her employment duties primarily from home, the home workspace is used more than 50% of the time for employment duties or the workspace is used exclusively to earn employment income and is used regularly and continuously for meeting customers or other persons in the normal course of business. The expenses can include a proportionate share of electricity, heat, cleaning materials, and minor repairs. If the employee rents the home or apartment, a proportionate share of the rent can be deducted. If the home is owned, there is no deduction for property taxes, home insurance, and mortgage payments. The expenses are only deductible up to the amount of the individual's employment income, and if there are excess expenses beyond that, the expenses can be carried forward indefinitely to be used against future income from the same employer.

- Legal expenses incurred to collect or establish a right to salary or wages owed to the individual by an employer or former employer. These expenses are not limited to the amount of income earned by the employee under his or her employment during the year — the expenses can be used to offset other sources of income. If there are no other sources of income, the loss can be a non-capital loss for the year.

- Tradespeople's and apprentice mechanics' tool expenses.

2. Business Deductions

Taxation of income in Canada requires that income be classified by its source (e.g., employment income, business income, capital gains). Distinguishing among the different sources of income is crucial because tax treatment varies depending on the source. For example:

- The calculation of net income from a business or property is different from the calculation of net income from employment because of the timing of income inclusions and the different types of deductions.

- The source of income determines the availability of certain tax credits (such as the foreign tax credit).

- Income from the disposition of property is taxed at a different rate depending on whether the income is classified as a capital gain or as business or property income.

It can be difficult to distinguish the difference between types of income. It is clear when someone is actively involved in a business or is a professional such as a lawyer, dentist, doctor, or chartered accountant — the nature of the activity is usually clear. However, when property is rented or sold, it may be unclear as to whether it was business property or investment property.

It is also sometimes difficult to determine if the business is a hobby or an actual business. There are certain tests in Canada to determine whether an activity will be considered a hobby or a business activity. The venture is considered to be a source of business income only if it is undertaken in a sufficiently commercial way. To be commercial in nature, there has to be an intention of earning profit and it must be run in a businesslike way. If there is a question about these tests, CRA will review an individual's venture and apply various criteria to provide evidence that either supports or refutes a claim of a venture being a business.

Because business income and property income are both undertaken in pursuit of profit, it is not easy to distinguish between the two types of income. If the income is passive, meaning it is derived from the ownership of the property and not the use of the property, it is generally classified as an investment and not a business activity. A rental activity can be determined to be either passive or active, depending on how involved a landlord is in the management of the property and how many services are provided to the tenants.

The classification of an individual's income as either employment income or self-employment income also determines what deductions can be taken. There are four tests to determine whether someone is self-employed (a contractor) or is an employee:

- **Control test:** How much control does the hirer have over the work to be performed?

- **Integration test:** How closely integrated are a worker's services to the business of the hirer?

- **Economic reality test:** What are the economic aspects of the relationship between the parties? There are several questions to consider including who profits from a contract, who covers operating costs, who covers workers' benefits, is there a guarantee of a minimum payment, does the individual's income fluctuate with the amount of work completed, etc.?

If it is determined that the income is business income, there are broad allowances for deductions. The starting point for analyzing the deductibility of a business expense is to determine if there is a "business criterion" for the general deductibility of expenses. The expenses must relate to the process of earning business income and must comply with ordinary and well-accepted principles of business practice.

Once it is determined that the basic criteria for deductibility has been satisfied, the next step is to ensure that the expense is not prohibited by a general or specific rule. The general limitations relating to the deductibility of expenses are as follows:

- The expense must be incurred to earn business income.
- The expense must not be on a capital account.
- The expense must be reasonable in the circumstances.

There are a number of specific limitations that restrict or prohibit the deduction of certain expenses. As an example, the following costs are not permitted as deductions:

- Personal and living expenses
- Expenses related to a provision, contingency, or a sinking fund
- Expenses for the use or maintenance of property that is a yacht, camp, lodge, golf course, or facility, unless the individual incurred the outlay or expense in the ordinary course of business of providing the property for rent
- Expenses related to income tax, penalties, interest, or fines
- Expenses related to political contributions

Taxable business income and expenses in Canada are determined using an accrual method of accounting, mostly according to generally accepted accounting principles (GAAP). This is different than the US that generally uses a cash basis method of accounting for determining taxable income. In the US, it is often possible to prepay expenses and get the taxable benefit for the payment in the year the payment is made. This cannot be accomplished using the accrual method; the expense can only be deducted when the taxpayer gets the related benefit. You should note, however, that this method of income recognition applies only to income and expenses related to profit generation (such as business income and property income) in Canada and does not apply to employment income-employment income and related expenses are determined based on a cash basis method of accounting.

2.1 Advertising expenses

All advertising expenses are deductible with certain restrictions for advertising in periodicals. Only 50% of advertising expenses can be deducted if the periodical is directed at a Canadian market and the editorial content is less than 80% of the issue's total non-advertising content. Advertising to a Canadian market from a non-Canadian broadcaster is not deductible.

2.2 Meals and entertainment

Only 50% of expenses for food, beverages, and entertainment can be deducted. If the expense is not reasonable, then only 50% of a reasonable expense can be deducted. There are certain exceptions to these rules, for example, a long-haul truck driver can deduct 80% of his or her expenses for food and beverages consumed while on the road.

2.3 Bad debts

Bad debts can be deducted if an account receivable is determined to be a bad debt during the year and if the amount was already included in income.

2.4 Insurance

All ordinary insurance premiums incurred for any part of your business can be deducted. There are restrictions on deducting motor vehicle insurance and home insurance expenses related to a home office. Life insurance is typically not deductible unless it is used as collateral for a loan to the business.

2.5 Interest

Interest is deductible when incurred on money borrowed for business purposes or to purchase business property. The deductible amount is limited when borrowing to purchase a passenger vehicle and when borrowing to purchase vacant land; you can only deduct interest up to the amount that the land generates income minus all other expenses without creating a loss.

2.6 Other loan costs

Fees paid to reduce a loan are deductible, as are penalties or bonuses that a financial institution charges for paying off a loan early, but the fees, penalties, or bonuses must be amortized and deducted over the remaining life of the original loan. Certain fees can be amortized over a five-year period and deducted over five years, regardless of the life of the loan. These are:

- Application, appraisal, processing, and insurance fees
- Loan guarantee fees
- Loan brokerage and finder's fees
- Legal fees for refinancing

If the loan is paid before the five-year period ends, the remaining balance that had not been deducted can be included in the year the loan is paid.

2.7 Salaries, wages, and bonuses

You can deduct salaries and other benefits paid to employees. However, you cannot deduct salaries or drawings that have been paid to you as the owner of the business reporting the income. Likewise, you cannot deduct payments to your partners. You can, however, deduct payments to your child as long as the payment is reasonable and the work is necessary to the business and is done by the child.

As the employer, you can deduct your part of CPP (Canadian Pension Plan) or (QPP (Quebec Pension Plan) contributions, EI (Employment Insurance) premiums, PPIP (Provincial Parental Insurance Plan) premiums available for residents of Quebec only, and Workers' Compensation amounts. You can deduct any insurance premiums paid for an employee.

2.8 Private health services premiums

A private health services plan is a tax-free vehicle for financing the healthcare costs of employees. You can deduct your own personal premiums paid if your net income from employment is greater than 50% of your total income; your income from sources other than self-employment income is less than $10,000 CAD; you are an active participant in your business; and the premiums paid are to insure you, your spouse, and/or any member of your household. If you do not have any employees, the deduction is limited to $1,500 CAD each for you and your spouse and $750 CAD for each other member of your household under the age of 18.

2.9 Motor vehicle expenses

The following chart (Chart A — Motor vehicle expenses) is used on page 6 of a CRA Form T2125 (Statement of Business or Professional Activities). The chart can help you calculate the amount of motor vehicle expenses that can be deducted. You should maintain very good records for the number of kilometers being driven for work or business purposes. The kind of vehicle you own can affect the deductibility of expenses. There are two categories of vehicles:

- **Motor vehicle:** This is an auto that is designed or adapted for use on highways or streets. It does not include a trolley, bus, or vehicle designed or adapted to be operated only on rails.

- **Passenger vehicle:** This is a motor vehicle that is designed or adapted for use on highways or streets as well and is designed primarily to carry no more than eight passengers. There may be a limit on the amount of capital cost allowance (CCA), interest, and leasing costs that you can deduct for a passenger vehicle. Passenger vehicles do not include ambulances; clearly marked fire, emergency, or police vehicles; taxis (or vehicles used more than 50% as a taxi); buses;

hearses; or vehicles purchased for inventory in sales, renting, or leasing activities.

The types of expenses that can be deducted include license and registration fees, fuel and oil costs, insurance, interest on money borrowed to purchase the vehicle, maintenance and repairs, and leasing costs. Only the expenses incurred to produce business income can be deducted, so if the vehicle is used for both personal and business purposes, you may need to pro-rate the expenses based on kilometers driven for each purpose. Again, you should maintain a very good log of your kilometers driven and the expenses incurred, and separate records should be kept for separate vehicles. The following is an example of the allocation of vehicle expenses.

John owns a plumbing business with a December 31 year-end. He has a van that he uses for the business. He recorded the following expenses during the year in his log:

License and registration fees	$ 200
Gas and oil	$ 3,000
Insurance	$ 2,000
Interest	$ 600
Maintenance and repairs	$ 400
Total expenses for the van	$ 6,200

John also logged the following kilometers driven:

Total kilometers driven to earn business income:	32,000
Total kilometers driven	36,000

The expenses that John can deduct for the year are calculated as follows:

(32,000 business kilometers)/(36,000 total kilometers) X 6,200=$5,511

John also incurred direct business expenses which were parking meter fees of $60 when he was providing plumbing services at a downtown location. The entire amount of the direct business expenses is deductible and does not have to be allocated.

Leasing costs for vehicles can be deducted, but are limited to $800 CAD per month before taxes (i.e., lease payments in excess of $800 before taxes are not deductible). Capital cost allowance cannot be deducted on vehicle costs in excess of $30,000 CAD before taxes. The calculation of the deductible amount is based on the lesser of two formulas — a basic cumulative formula that calculates the deductibility of lease payments to $800 plus GST/HST and PST for each 30-day period the lease is in effect during the year, and an anti-avoidance formula that uses the manufacturer's list price and a standard 15% discount. These two formulas are rather complicated and can be calculated by completing "Chart C — Eligible leasing costs for passenger vehicles" on page 6 of Form T2125.

Capital cost allowance (CCA) on vehicles can also be deducted and is discussed later in this chapter.

2.10 Other expenses

Other expenses that can be deducted in the normal course of business include office expenses, supplies, legal and accounting fees, other professional fees, management and administration fees, rent, maintenance and repairs, property taxes, travel expenses related to the business, telephone and utility costs, fuel costs except for motor vehicles, and delivery and freight costs. You can also deduct expenses related to modifications to make your property wheelchair accessible. If you lease computer equipment, cellular telephones, or other equipment, you can deduct the lease costs that reasonably relate to your business (but if you purchase the equipment, you cannot deduct the cost but instead can deduct CCA). You can deduct the costs of attending two conventions per year as long as the conventions relate to your business or professional activity and the conventions are held in an area where you usually do business (note, however, that any meals or entertainment are limited to 50%).

2.11 Capital cost allowance

The US uses a depreciation system as its cost-recovery vehicle for capital investments. In Canada, there is a similar system that allows for a deduction which is known as a capital cost allowance or CCA. The CCA system is the tax equivalent of accounting for capital assets, including depreciation. It deals with acquisition, useful life, disposition, gain or loss on disposal, obsolescence, destruction, improvements as opposed to repairs and maintenance, and so forth. The purpose of this discussion is not to give you all of the details of the capital cost allowance methodology; it is instead to provide you with a primer on how expenses for CCA are available for capital assets. An entire chapter could have been devoted to the intricacies of capital assets and CCA.

There are no capital cost recovery deductions allowed for personal use assets, only for business use assets. CCA can be deducted as an expense in computing an individual's business and professional net income or net rental income. In limited circumstances, CCA can be claimed as an employment-related expense as mentioned previously in this chapter.

CRA provides guidelines to determine what property constitutes capital property as compared to a maintenance or repair expense. There is not a simple answer to the question in either Canada or the US. The criteria used by CRA are as follows:

- Does the expense provide a lasting benefit? CRA provides an example that painting the wood on the exterior of a wooden building does not provide a lasting benefit, but putting vinyl siding on the building is a lasting improvement and would be added to the capital cost of the building.

- Does the expense maintain or improve the property? CRA provides the example of a repair of an existing set of wooden steps versus replacing the steps with concrete steps. The concrete steps would be a capital improvement versus an expenditure.

- Is the expense for a part of the property or is it a separate asset? CRA provides an example of how replacing wiring in a building is normally an expense, but buying a compressor for a business is a separate addition and a capital asset.

Property is typically separated into classes, and each class of property is depreciated based on criteria set forth by CRA for each asset class. The following table provides a brief property list and classes of property subject to depreciation. There are over 40 classes of property; we are showing only the most common in Table 17.

When a property is sold, you may have to add any undepreciated capital cost as recapture of CCA to your income or you may be able to take a deduction as a terminal loss. You should also take note that there is a CCA restriction on rental property of an individual or partnership: CCA cannot be claimed on a rental property to increase rental losses.

2.12 Lifetime capital gains deduction

An individual who is a resident of Canada throughout the year is entitled to a lifetime cumulative capital gains deduction (or exemption) of $824,176 CAD (2016) for dispositions after March 2007. Since only one-half of the capital gain is taxable, the resulting lifetime capital gain deduction limit is $412,088. This applies only to capital gains realized on the disposition of qualified farm or fishing property and qualified small business corporation stock.

A share of a corporation is considered to be a qualified Canadian-controlled small-business corporation share if all of the following conditions are met:

- At the time of the disposition, the share was a share of the capital stock of a small business corporation and the share was owned by the individual, the individual's spouse, or a partnership of which the individual was a partner.

- The shares must not be owned by anyone other than the taxpayer or related person for at least 24 months preceding the disposition.

Table 17
COMMONLY USED CCA CLASSES

Class of Property	Rates
Class 1 – Buildings. This includes bridges and canals	A 4% rate is used for buildings acquired after 1987. A 10% rate is used if the property is used 90% or more for manufacturing, and a 6% rate if it is used 90% or more for non-residential purposes other than manufacturing
Class 3 – Buildings acquired before 1988	5% declining balance
Class 8 – Machinery, equipment and furniture. This includes refrigerators, appliances, kilns, tanks, vats, electrical generating equipment. It can include furniture if not specified in another class	20% declining balance
Class 10 – Vehicles. This is most vehicles including trailers and wagons	30% declining balance
Class 12 – Computer software and small assets	100%
Class 13 – Leasehold improvements. The term is the remaining lease term which is limited to 40 years and can be no less than 5 years	Straight-line based on the term of the lease
Class 14 – Intangible assets	Straight-line
Class 29– Manufacturing and Processing Assets acquired after March 18, 2007	50% declining balance
Class 44 – Patents	25% declining balance
Class 50 – Computer Hardware and Systems Software	55% declining balance

- More than 50% of the fair market value of the corporation's assets must be used in an active business carried on primarily in Canada for the 24 months preceding the disposition.

- The corporation cannot be controlled directly or indirectly by one or more nonresident persons.

- The corporation cannot be controlled directly or indirectly by one or more public companies, nor is it controlled by a Canadian resident corporation that lists its shares on a designated stock exchange outside of Canada.

- No class of its shares are listed on a stock exchange.

The capital gains exemption has changed numerous times since it was first introduced as a $500,000 capital gains exemption on all capital gains. It was criticized as a gift to higher income Canadians and as a result, it was then limited to stock of Canadian-Controlled Private Corporations. It is currently indexed for inflation and started at an $824,176 exemption amount in 2016.

2.13 Qualified farm property and qualified fishing property

Qualified farm property is real property used more than 50% in a farming business, shares of a farm corporation, an interest in a family farm partnership, and certain eligible capital property used principally in a farming business like milk and egg quotas. Qualified fishing property includes real property, fishing vessels, and eligible capital property used primarily in a fishing business carried on in Canada in which the taxpayer or his or her spouse, parent, child, or grandchild was actively engaged in a regular and continuous basis. It also includes capital stock of a family fishing corporation or partnership. The exemption for qualified farm or fishing property is an additional $175,824 CAD, for a total exemption of $1,000,000.

3. Other Personal Deductions

3.1 RRSP contributions

Each taxpayer may deduct RRSP contributions made in the year and up to 60 days following the end of the year subject to the taxpayer's RRSP deduction limit for the year (the lesser of 18% of the taxpayer's earned income for two years prior [2014 for a 2016 contribution] or $26,010 [2016 limit adjusted for inflation each year]). In addition, the deduction limit includes contribution room that is carried from all previous years from unfunded contributions in those years. The taxpayer can, thus, contribute up to the current year limit plus any carried forward contribution room, and the contribution will be fully tax deductible.

3.2 Split pension amount

Canadian taxpayers cannot file joint returns with their spouses. In many cases, one spouse earns significantly more than another spouse resulting in one spouse's income being taxed at a higher tax rate than the lower income spouse's income. Income splitting between spouses is one of the most effective tax savings techniques that can be used by individual taxpayers because of this inequity. CRA recognized this inequity when it relates to couples who earn a pension. Any Canadian taxpayer who receives an eligible pension can file a joint election with a spouse to reallocate up to 50% of the pension to his or her spouse. A deduction is allowed for the pensioner for 50% of the pension which is also reported as income on the spouse's income tax return. For individuals 65 or older, this income includes annuity payments from a registered pension plan, RRSP, deferred profit sharing plan, and registered income fund payments.

3.3 Child care expenses

The *Income Tax Act* provides for a deduction for child care expenses paid to third parties. If there is more than one supporting person, the deduction generally must be reported on the return of the person with the lowest net income. The child must be 16 or under and not have income in excess of the basic personal credit amount ($11,474 CAD for 2016). The deduction is limited to the lower of the actual expenses paid for child care services, the deduction limit, or 2/3 of the taxpayer's earned income. The deduction limit is $8,000 for each child under the age of seven at the end of the year and $5,000 for each child between 7 and 15 years of age during the year. If the child is eligible for a disability tax credit, the deduction limit is $11,000 CAD with no age requirement.

3.4 Disability support

A deduction is allowed for disability support expenses incurred for education or employment purposes to be fully tax deductible, rather than being limited to claims under the nonrefundable medical expenses tax credit. The deduction is restricted to amounts paid for eligible devices and services and is limited in deductibility.

This is the first of several disability-related tax measures available to persons with disabilities, as well as to persons supporting them.

Many of these deductions and credits interact with each other, so an individual with a disability or who supports a person with a disability should consider the availability of each of these tax measures and choose the most advantageous combination. For example, the disability supports deduction can be taken in conjunction with the disability tax credit and the refundable medical expense supplement. However, an individual must choose between a medical expenses tax credit or a disability supports deduction when he or she has paid disability support expenses during the year.

3.5 Moving expenses

Eligible relocation expenses are deductible in Canada when moving to a new location for employment or to carry on business. Both the residence that you are leaving and the residence you are moving to must be in Canada, and the new residence must be at least 40 kilometers closer to the individual's new work location than the old residence. The expenses cannot exceed employment income or business income earned at the new location for the year, which can be problematic if the move happens late in the year. However, any expenses that exceed the threshold limit can be carried over to the next year. There are limitations on what constitutes eligible relocation expenses,

Table 18
DISABILITY-RELATED TAX MEASURES

Available to persons with disabilities	Available to persons supporting persons with disabilities
Disability supports deduction	Child care expenses deduction
Disability tax credit (including a supplement for persons under 18)	Infirm dependent tax credit
Medical expenses tax credit for the individual	Caregiver tax credit
Refundable medical expense supplement	Disability tax credit transferred from a dependent
	Disability tax credit transferred from a spouse or common-law partner
	Medical expenses tax credit for spouse or common-law partner and dependents
	Children's fitness tax credit
	Refundable medical expense supplement

but most expenses directly related to a move, during the time of the move, are deductible by an individual taxpayer as long as they are not reimbursed by an employer.

Note: A move from the US to Canada is not deductible by an individual. We suggest that you have your employer pay the cost of moving from the US if that is at all possible.

3.6 Spousal and child support payments

Spousal support payments are handled similarly in Canada as in the US. They are deductible from the paying spouse's income in the year they are paid and are reported as income for the receiving spouse. Child support is neither taxable nor deductible.

3.7 Deduction for foreign non-business income tax

Foreign tax credits are discussed in Chapter 5 of this book. However, as an alternative to claiming foreign tax as a tax credit, an individual may be allowed to claim the tax as a deduction. The qualifications of a foreign tax are the same as discussed in Chapter 5. Because the foreign tax credit is limited to taxes paid up to a rate of 15%, the only other option for the foreign non-business income tax paid by an individual in excess of 15% is to take the deduction for the excess foreign tax paid.

3.8 Other deductions

There are a limited number of other deductions available for Canadian taxpayers including:

- Deduction for Provincial Parental Insurance Plan (PPIP) premiums on self-employment income (this is available for self-employed residents of Quebec).

- Deduction for CPP or QPP contributions on self-employment income or business or professional income from a partnership.

- Legal fees incurred in appealing a tax assessment, to collect a retirement allowance or pension benefit, or to collect support payments from a spouse.

4. Nonrefundable Tax Credits

Nonrefundable tax credits are those credits that are only available up to the extent that an individual has federal tax. Only a few of the credits are able to be carried over if they are not used in the current year (which are the tax credits for unused tuition, education, and textbook amounts; donations and gifts; investments; and interest paid on student loans). If several credits apply, there is a specific order by which the credits can be applied — the individual does not have a choice to use one credit over another. These credits are listed in order in this section of this chapter.

Just because a credit is listed here does not mean that you get a full credit. With the exception of the donations and gifts credit, the overseas employment tax credit, the federal foreign tax credit, and the federal dividend credit, all other credits are multiplied by an applicable rate which is currently 15% (the lowest federal marginal tax rate).

For nonresidents, residency status determines which nonrefundable tax credits they can claim. If all or substantially all (90% or more) of an individual's net world income is Canadian-source income, then he or she can have all of the credits available to him or her. Otherwise, only the following credits may be claimed:

- CPP and QPP credits
- Employment insurance credit
- Disability credit
- Interest paid on student loans credit
- Tuition credit
- Donations and gifts credit

That is unless a nonresident elects under section 217 to report his or her Canadian benefit payments (which include payments from pensions, death benefits, registered retirement accounts, government assistance programs, unemployment, and other similar type benefits) on a T1 return; then he or she may claim all of the nonrefundable tax credits that apply to him or her.

For a resident who is only a part-year resident, the tax credits may be prorated for the number of days in the tax year during which the individual is resident in Canada, or fully available to the extent the credits relate to the period of residency. Table 19 shows which category applies to each of the credits.

Table 19
CREDITS AND PRORATING

Credits that usually need to be prorated	Credits that are claimed in full without proration
Basic personal credit	CPP and QPP credits
Age credit	Employment insurance credit
Spouse or common law partner credit	Adoption expenses credit
Eligible dependent credit	Pension income credit
Inform dependent credit	Interest paid on student loans credit
Caregiver credit	Tuition credit
Disability credit	Education credit
Tuition, education, and textbook credits transferred from a child	Textbook credit
Credits transferred from a spouse or common-law partner	Medical expenses credit
	Donations and gifts credit
	Canada employment credit
	Public transit passes credit
	Child fitness credit
	Quebec parental insurance plan credits

4.1 Basic personal credit

Every individual is entitled to claim the basic personal amount of $11,474 for 2016, which results in a tax credit of $1,721 ($11,474 multiplied by the applicable rate of 15%). This amount is indexed each year.

4.2 Spouse or common-law partner credit

The maximum amount of $11,474 (2016) is available to an individual where the net income of his or her spouse is below a net income threshold and the individual supports the spouse. If the spouse's income is less than the maximum amount, then the credit is limited to the actual amount of income. The applicable rate of 15% applies, so the maximum credit is $1,721.

4.3 Eligible dependent credit

The credit for an eligible dependent is also referred to as the wholly dependent person credit and may be claimed for a wholly dependent person who was not already claimed for a spouse or common-law partner credit. The maximum amount for 2016 is $11,474 (which results in a credit of $1,721) and is reduced for the wholly dependent person's net income. An eligible dependent (or wholly dependent person) is either:

- an individual's parent or grandparent by blood, marriage, common-law partnership, or adoption, or

- an individual's child, grandchild, brother or sister by blood, married, common-law partnership, or adoption, and is either under 18 or mentally or physically infirm.

The dependent must be a resident of Canada unless the claim is for the individual's child.

4.4 Infirm dependent credit

A claim of $6,788 (for 2016) is available only when the dependent's net income is below a threshold of $6,807 (for 2016). Therefore, the maximum credit for 2015 would be $1,018. A credit can be claimed for an eligible dependent person who is infirm and relies wholly on the taxpayer for support. Eligible dependent persons include children, grandchildren, parents, grandparents, brothers, sisters, uncles, aunts, nieces, and nephews.

4.5 Caregiver credit

This is one of the disability-related tax measures. To qualify for the caregiver amount (also known as the in-home care of relative amount), an individual must have maintained a self-contained domestic establishment where both the individual and the person for whom the taxpayer is making the claim lived at some time during the year. The maximum claim is $4,667 for 2016 (the credit is $700) and is available if the dependent's income does not exceed a threshold of $15,940 (2016).

4.6 Universal child care benefit

This was new in 2015 and replaced what was formerly a child tax credit. Instead of providing a tax credit for each child, a taxable benefit is now paid out to help Canadian families balance work and family life to pay for child care benefits. The benefit for 2015 was $160 per month per child and paid out for all children up through the age of 17. In order to qualify for the benefit, you must live with the child and be a Canadian resident. Either you or your spouse must be a Canadian citizen, permanent resident, or have lived continuously in Canada for the preceding 18 months as a temporary resident. Payments are issued by the Canadian government on the 20th of each month.

Note: The 2016 Budget is replacing the Universal Child Care Benefit (UCCB) and Canada Child Tax Benefit (CCTB) with a new Canada Child Benefit (CCB) that provides monthly tax-free benefits that are tied to income.

4.7 Age credit

A credit is available for individuals who reach the age of 65 before the end of the year. The amount is $7,125 for 2016 which results in a credit of $1,069 ($7,125 x 15%).

4.8 CPP and QPP credits

A tax credit equal to 15% of the CPP or QPP contributions paid on employment income and half of the CPP or QPP contributions paid on self-employment income.

4.9 Employment Insurance (EI) credit

A tax credit is also available that is equal to 15% of the employment insurance premiums paid by an individual.

4.10 Pension income credit

A tax credit is available for 15% of the first $2,000 of eligible pension income including income from Old Age Security (OAS) or CPP/QPP, provincial pension plans, salary deferral arrangements, retirement compensation arrangements, employee benefit plans, and death benefits.

4.11 Canada employment credit

An individual who reports employment income on his or her T1 can claim up to $1,161 (for 2016). The credit is a maximum of $174.

4.12 Volunteer firefighters' and volunteer search and rescue credit

If an individual volunteers as a firefighter or a search and rescue worker for a minimum of 200 hours during a tax year, he or she is eligible for a credit of 15% of $3,000. In addition, there is an exemption for up to $1,000 of compensation received for these types of volunteer work.

4.13 Adoption expenses credit

The *Income Tax Act* provides for a tax credit for eligible adoption expenses, up to a maximum of $15,453 for 2016. The maximum credit is $2,318 ($15,453 x 15%).

4.14 Public transit passes credit

The cost of passes for public transportation within Canada can be claimed for you, your spouse, and your children under 19 years of age at the beginning of the year. The credit is equal to 15% of the cost.

4.15 Children's fitness credit

You can claim up to $1,000 per child for the costs of registration or membership for your child in a program of physical activity. The child must either be 16 and under at the beginning of the year or 18 and under if the child qualifies for the disability credit as well. This results in a maximum credit of $150 (15% of $1,500) per child.

4.16 Children's arts credit

You can claim up to $500 per child for the costs of registration or membership for your child in a cultural, recreational, or development activity, plus an additional $500 if the child is disabled. This results in a maximum credit of $75 ($500 x 15%) per child.

4.17 Disability credit

A credit of $1,200 (15% x $8,001 for 2016) is available for a disabled individual or a dependent. If the disabled person is a minor under the age of 18, an additional credit of $700 (15% x $4,667 for 2016) is also available.

4.18 Medical expenses credit

The medical expenses credit is one of several tax measures available to individuals who incur significant medical-related expenses either for themselves, their spouses or common-law partners, or their dependents. There is a broad listing of allowable medical expenses. The credit is equal to 15% of the amount of medical expenses paid in excess of the lesser of 3% of the individual's net income or $2,237 (2016).

4.19 Home buyer's credit

You can claim $5,000 for the purchase of a home located in Canada that you intend to occupy as long as the home is being purchased by your or your spouse and you or your spouse did not live in another home owned by you or your spouse in the year of acquisition or in any of the four preceding years. The corresponding credit is $750 (15% of $5,000).

4.20 Donations and gifts credit

An individual who has made a charitable gift to a registered charity or other qualifying entity may be entitled to claim a donations and gifts tax credit. There are annual limits to the allowable gift, and the non-refundable tax credit is equal to 15% of the first $200 of donations and 29% on donations in excess of this amount.

Gifts of capital property are considered disposed of in the year gifted and are taxed to the donor on the capital gain. The credit for gifts of cash or other property to a registered charity is generally limited to 75% of your net income for the year. However, you can increase your total donations limit if you donate capital property which can be determined only through a calculation of the effect of the capital gain, net of the deduction, on your net income. Also, if the donations exceed the 75% limit or if you choose to do so, you can carry forward the charitable donations for five years.

A one-time First-Time Donor's Super Credit (FDSC) is available to first-time donors. The credit is equal to 25% of up to $1,000 in eligible donations (couples must share the $1,000 limit).

4.21 Interest paid on student loans credit

If a student or a related person paid interest on a student loan, a credit for the student equal to 15% of the interest paid in the year or the previous five years (if not already claimed in those years) is available.

4.22 Federal dividend credit

Canada has an integrated system of taxation between corporations and their shareholders to minimize a double tax situation resulting from tax paid on income by a corporation and then being paid again by the individual shareholder when dividends are issued. Dividends received by a shareholder are "grossed up," or increased by a factor to reflect the amount of income that was received by the corporation before it paid tax. The grossed up amount is included in the taxpayer's income. A credit is then provided to the individual taxpayer which compensates for the taxes that were paid at the corporate level.

This credit is not reduced by the applicable amount (15%). The rates of gross-up and the credit amounts are determined annually based on corporate tax rates. Also, there are separate rates for eligible dividends (dividends paid by corporations that are generally public Canadian companies and are not Canadian-controlled private companies) and non-eligible dividends (Canadian-controlled private companies).

Eligible dividends are grossed up by 38% and the corresponding dividend is 6/11 of the gross-up amount.

Table 20
NON-ELIGIBLE DIVIDEND GROSS-UP PERCENTAGES
AND TAX CREDITS

	2015	2016	2017	2018	2019
Gross-up percentage	18%	17%	17%	16%	15%
Dividend Tax Credit (as a percentage of the grossed up dividends)	13/18 or 72.22%	21/29 or 72.41%	20/29 or 68.97%	20/20 or 68.97%	9/13 or 69.23%

According to the Department of Finance Canada Budget 2015, non-eligible dividends received by an individual will be grossed up by a factor of 17% for 2016 and 2017, 16% for 2018, and 15% beginning in 2019, and the corresponding dividend tax credit will be 21/29 of the grossed-up amount for 2016, 20/29 for 2017 and 2018, and 9/13 for 2019.

4.23 Overseas employment tax credit

An individual who is a resident of Canada but works outside of Canada may reduce tax payable if he or she qualifies for the overseas employment tax credit (OETC). The individual qualifies for the OETC if he or she remains a resident of Canada; is employed outside of Canada for more than six consecutive months that begin before the end of the year and includes any part of the year; is employed by a Canadian employer, substantially all (at least 90%) of his or her duties are outside of Canada; and is employed for specific purposes of resource exploration or exploitation, construction or engineering activity, or other prescribed activity. The OETC is a direct deduction from tax payable on up to $80,000 of an individual's income from his or her OETC duties.

Note: The OETC was scheduled to be phased out as of December 31, 2015. However, if you had qualifying foreign employment income in connection with a contract that your employer committed to in writing before March 29, 2012, the phase-out will not apply.

4.24 Federal foreign tax credit

Foreign tax credits are more fully discussed in Chapter 5. You should note, however, that foreign tax credits are the last in the line of nonrefundable tax credits. The tax credits must be applied in order. As non-business income foreign tax credits can only be used in the year the foreign taxes are levied, the ordering of credits, with foreign tax credits being applied last, increases the likelihood of not having sufficient Canadian income tax payable to fully utilize foreign tax credits.

5. Refundable Tax Credits

Up to this point, we have discussed credits that could not result in a refund to the taxpayer. There are a few credits that are refundable, meaning that they can be applied to reduce the total tax to less than zero, and the negative tax balance would be refunded to the taxpayer. These are typically overpayments of tax or other government payments of items such as overpaid CPP/QPP contributions and EI contributions. The following refundable credits are also available.

5.1 Refundable medical expenses

You can claim a credit for medical expenses up to $1,187 if you were a Canadian resident for the full year and your earned income is greater than $3,465 for the year. The family net income threshold is $26,277.

5.2 Refundable GST/HST credit

If you deduct expenses on your income as an employee or as a partner, you may be eligible for a rebate of the GST/HST you pay on those expenses. The amount of credit is calculated by the CRA on the basis of information included on your tax return for a particular year, and the credit is automatically paid to you in a subsequent year. For payments from July 2015 to June 2016, the basic GST/HST credit for an individual is $272. For families, the credit is $272 for you and $272 for your spouse or common-law partner (or other parent of your child). An eligible child will be credited with $143. There's also a GST/HST supplement credit of up to $143 for certain low-income single persons and single parents. If you live with your spouse or common-law partner (or other parent of your child), only one of you may claim the credit for the family unit, and it doesn't matter which of you claims the credit.

However, the total credit you may claim is reduced by 5% of your combined adjusted net incomes for 2014 in excess of a specified threshold, which is currently $35,465 (this amount is adjusted annually for inflation). Therefore, a married couple with two eligible children qualifies for the full credit of $830 if their combined family income is $35,465 or less. Their entitlement decreases to zero once family income exceeds $52,065.

Table 21 shows the credit available for the period July 2015 to June 2016 (2014 tax year). New residents of Canada can apply for the GST/HST credit in the year that they become residents of Canada, using the Canada Revenue Agency (CRA) Form RC151: GST/HST Credit Application for Individuals Who Become Residents of Canada.

5.3 Working income credit

This credit is available for very low income individuals and is equal to 25% of an individual's working income in excess of $3,000. It is reduced to 15% when working income reaches $11,525 ($15,915 for couples) and phases out completely when working income reaches $18,292 ($28,208 for couples). The credit cannot exceed $1,015 for individuals or $1,844 for a family.

Table 21
GST/HST CREDITS: JULY 2015 – JUNE 2016 (TAX YEAR 2014)

Single

Family net income ($)	No children ($/year)	1 child ($/year)	2 children ($/year)	3 children ($/year)	4 children ($/year)
under 8,833	272.00	687.00	830.00	973.00	1,116.00
10,000	295.34	687.00	830.00	973.00	1,116.00
15,000	395.34	687.00	830.00	973.00	1,116.00
20,000	415.00	687.00	830.00	973.00	1,116.00
25,000	415.00	687.00	830.00	973.00	1,116.00
30,000	415.00	687.00	830.00	973.00	1,116.00
35,000	415.00	687.00	830.00	973.00	1,116.00
36,000	388.25	660.25	803.25	946.25	1,089.25
37,000	328.25	610.25	753.25	896.25	1,039.25
38,000	288.25	560.25	703.25	846.25	989.25
39,000	238.25	510.25	653.25	796.25	939.25
40,000	188.25	460.25	603.25	746.25	889.25
42,000	88.25	360.25	503.25	646.25	789.25
44,000	0.00	260.25	403.25	546.25	689.25
46,000	0.00	160.25	303.25	446.25	589.25
48,000	0.00	60.25	203.25	346.25	489.25
50,000	0.00	0.00	103.25	246.25	389.25
52,000	0.00	0.00	3.25	146.25	289.25
54,000	0.00	0.00	0.00	46.25	189.25
56,000	0.00	0.00	0.00	0.00	89.25
58,000	0.00	0.00	0.00	0.00	0.00

Table 21 — Continued

Married

Family net income ($)	No children ($/year)	1 child ($/year)	2 children ($/year)	3 children ($/year)	4 children ($/year)
under 35,000	544.00	687.00	830.00	973.00	1,116.00
36,000	517.25	660.25	803.25	946.25	1,089.25
37,000	467.25	610.25	753.25	896.25	1,039.25
38,000	417.25	560.25	703.25	846.25	989.25
39,000	367.25	510.25	653.25	796.25	939.25
40,000	317.25	460.25	603.25	746.25	889.25
42,000	217.25	360.25	503.25	646.25	789.25
44,000	117.25	260.25	403.25	546.25	689.25
46,000	17.25	160.25	303.25	446.25	589.25
48,000	0.00	60.25	203.25	346.25	489.25
50,000	0.00	0.00	103.25	246.25	389.25
52,000	0.00	0.00	3.25	146.25	289.25
54,000	0.00	0.00	0.00	46.25	189.25
56,000	0.00	0.00	0.00	0.00	89.25
58,000	0.00	0.00	0.00	0.00	0.00

Notes:

1. The amounts listed above represent yearly entitlements for the GST/HST credit based on marital status, family size, and net income.

2. The yearly entitlement for the 2014 tax year is paid in 4 quarterly issuances in the months of July and October 2015 and January and April 2016.

3. These amounts are only to be used as a guideline.

4. All recipients must keep the Canada Revenue Agency informed of any changes to their current address, family size and marital situation.

5. The universal child care benefit (UCCB) and/or registered disability savings plan (RDSP) are not be included as part of your adjusted family net income in the calculation of your GST/HST credit.

* Source: http://www.cra-arc.gc.ca/bnfts/gstc_pymnt14-eng.html

Table 22
SUMMARY OF 2016 NONREFUNDABLE PERSONAL TAX CREDITS

Tax Credit Type	Base Amount	Federal Credit Amount @ 15%
Basic personal amount	$11,474	$1,721
Spouse or common-law partner	$11,474	$1,721
Age 65+	$7,125	$1,069
Disability	$8,001	$1,200
Disability for taxpayers under age 18	$4,667	$700
Caregiver	$4,667	$700
Infirm dependent age 18+	$6,788	$1,018
Pension income — lesser of eligible pension income or	$2,000	$300
Medical expense (in excess of the lesser of 3% of net income)	$2,237	No limit
Canada employment	$1,161	$174
Eligible adoption expense (per child)	$15,453	$2,318

9

Tax Planning

Since Americans who are residents of Canada have to report their world income on both their US and Canadian tax returns, there are a multitude of foreign reporting forms that incur large penalties for late filing or non-filing of these forms. These reporting forms are essential to the taxing authorities of Canada and the US to ensure that a taxpayer's world income is being reported on his or her Canadian and US returns.

1. The Direction Your Planning Should Take

As an American in Canada, tax planning consists primarily of reducing your Canadian tax. Because you will normally have to file US and Canadian returns, and due to the effect of foreign tax credits and the Treaty, you will effectively be paying the tax of the higher-tax country. Because taxes are higher in Canada than they are in the US, your tax planning should be geared towards reducing your Canadian tax. In general, here is an example of how the interplay between the two countries will work, ignoring the currency exchange:

Base Case

$80,000 taxable income

$30,000 gross tax due to Canada

$20,000 tax due to the US

Canada will allow the $20,000 tax paid to the US as a foreign tax credit.

Net tax to Canada is $10,000 ($30,000 – $20,000)

Net tax to the US is $20,000

Total tax is $30,000

Reduce US Tax

$80,000 taxable income

$30,000 gross tax due to Canada

$15,000 tax due to the US

Canada will allow the $15,000 tax paid to the US as a foreign tax credit

Net tax to Canada is $15,000 ($30,000 - $15,000)

Net tax to the US is $15,000

Total tax is still $30,000 (notice that although the US tax declined, your total tax did not)

Reduce Canadian Tax

$80,000 taxable income

$25,000 gross tax due to Canada

$20,000 tax due to the US

Canada will allow the $20,000 tax paid to the US as a foreign tax credit.

Net tax to Canada is $5,000 ($25,000 - $20,000)

Net tax to the US is $20,000

Total tax is $25,000 (notice that although the US tax remained the same as example 1, your total tax declined because your Canadian tax declined)

There are unusual situations in which the US tax could be higher, such as selling a principal residence. If you sell a principal residence that has more than a $250,000 gain for a single taxpayer, or $500,000 for married taxpayers, you will have a taxable gain in the US but no tax in Canada.

An important part in any tax planning is considering the complexity and making sure all of the necessary tax forms are filed on time. Before we go into tax planning in any more detail we want to familiarize you with some basic tax filing requirements and forms required.

2. US Foreign Account Filing Requirements

Americans resident in Canada have to report annually with the Financial Crimes and Enforcement Network, FinCEN, via Form 114. This form is used to report a financial interest in or a signatory authority over a foreign financial account. This form has to be filed independently of the US tax return and has to be filed (electronically only). The form has traditionally been due on June 30 of the following year and no extensions had been allowed. The filing date has been changed for the 2016 tax year to April 15 and extensions will be allowed to October 15. At the time of the writing of this book, it is unclear as to whether a separate extension will be required or if the extension required for your individual income tax return will be sufficient. A US person that has a financial interest or a signature authority over financial accounts must file the FinCen114 if the aggregate value of all foreign financial accounts exceeds $10,000 at any time during the calendar year. In addition to the FinCen114 form taxpayers may also be required to file IRS Form 8938, Statement of Specified Foreign Financial Assets. Form 8938 is required for Americans in Canada when:

- Single taxpayers and married taxpayers filing as separate with foreign financial assets more than $200,000 on the last day of the year or $300,000 at any time during the year.

- Married taxpayers with foreign financial assets of more than $400,000 on the last day of the year or $600,000 at any time during the year.

Specified foreign assets would include not only bank accounts but also investment accounts, Registered Retirement Savings Plans, Registered Education Savings Plans, Tax-Free Savings Accounts, interests in foreign corporations, and foreign estates and trusts, as well as foreign deferred compensation plans.

2.1 If you own a Canadian corporation

Many Americans move to Canada and set up a business. IRS Form 5471 — Information Return of US Persons With Respect to Certain Foreign Corporations is required to be filed when a US person is an officer or director of a foreign corporation owns 10% or more of the value or votes of the stock of the foreign corporation or controls the foreign corporation. Form 5471 and its schedules are included with the taxpayer's 1040 return. Penalties for late filing are $10,000 as well as criminal penalties for willful conduct.

As a Canadian resident, you can set up a Canadian corporation to own a business you operate or hold your investments. The earnings are taxed within the Canadian corporation. However, the income earned within the Canadian corporation may or may not be taxable in the US, regardless of whether you paid yourself a dividend.

Without going into the complicated rules in detail, if the corporation is operating an active business, the income is deferred in the US until either money is withdrawn as a dividend, or the business is no longer operating. The opposite of this is that if you have a corporation holding your investments (investment portfolio, Guaranteed Investment Contracts, etc.) the

Table 23
COMPARISON OF FORM 8938 AND FBAR REQUIREMENTS

The Form 8938 filing requirement does not replace or otherwise affect a taxpayer's obligation to file FinCEN Form 114 (Report of Foreign Bank and Financial Accounts). Individuals must file each form for which they meet the relevant reporting threshold.

	Form 8938, Statement of Specified Foreign Financial Assets	FinCEN Form 114, Report of Foreign Bank and Financial Accounts (FBAR)
Who Must File?	Specified individuals, which include US citizens, resident aliens, and certain nonresident aliens that have an interest in specified foreign financial assets and meet the reporting threshold.	US persons, which include US citizens, resident aliens, trusts, estates, and domestic entities that have an interest in foreign financial accounts and meet the reporting threshold.
Reporting Threshold (Total Value of Assets)	$200,000 on the last day of the tax year or $300,000 at any time during the tax year (higher threshold amounts apply to married individuals filing jointly and individuals living abroad).	$10,000 at any time during the calendar year.
When Do You Have an Interest in an Account or Asset?	If any income, gains, losses, deductions, credits, gross proceeds, or distributions from holding or disposing of the account or asset are or would be required to be reported, included, or otherwise reflected on your income tax return.	Financial interest: You are the owner of record or holder of legal title; the owner of record or holder of legal title is your agent or representative; you have a sufficient interest in the entity that is the owner of record or holder of legal title. Signature authority: You have authority to control the disposition of the assets in the account by direct communication with the financial institution maintaining the account.
What Is Reported?	Maximum value of specified foreign financial assets, which include financial accounts with foreign financial institutions and certain other foreign non-account investment assets.	Maximum value of financial accounts maintained by a financial institution physically located in a foreign country.

Table 23 — Continued

How Are Maximum Account or Asset Values Determined and Reported?	Fair market value in US dollars in accord with the Form 8938 instructions for each account and asset reported. Convert to US dollars using the end of the taxable year exchange rate and report in US dollars.	Use periodic account statements to determine the maximum value in the currency of the account. Convert to US dollars using the end of the calendar year exchange rate and report in US dollars.
When Due?	By due date, including extension, if any, for income tax return.	Received by June 30 (no extensions of time granted).
Where to File?	File with income tax return pursuant to instructions for filing the return.	File electronically through FinCENs BSA E-Filing System. The FBAR is not filed with your federal tax return.
Penalties	Up to $10,000 for failure to disclose and an additional $10,000 for each 30 days of non-filing after IRS notice of a failure to disclose, for a potential maximum penalty of $60,000; criminal penalties may also apply.	If non-willful, up to $10,000; if willful, up to the greater of $100,000 or 50% of account balances; criminal penalties may also apply.
Types of Foreign Assets and Whether They are Reportable		
Financial (Deposit and Custodial) Accounts Held at Foreign Financial Institutions	Yes	Yes
Financial Account Held at a Foreign Branch of a US Financial Institution	No	Yes
Financial Account Held at a US Branch of a Foreign Financial Institution	No	No

Table 23 — Continued

Foreign Financial Account for Which You Have Signature Authority	No, unless you otherwise have an interest in the account as described above.	Yes, subject to exceptions.
Foreign Stock or Securities Held in a Financial Account at a Foreign Financial Institution	The account itself is subject to reporting, but the contents of the account do not have to be separately reported.	The account itself is subject to reporting, but the contents of the account do not have to be separately reported.
Foreign Stock or Securities not Held in a Financial Account	Yes	No
Foreign Partnership Interests	Yes	No
Indirect Interests in Foreign Financial Assets through an Antity	No	Yes, if sufficient ownership or beneficial interest (i.e., a greater than 50% interest) in the entity. See instructions for further detail.
Foreign Mutual Funds	Yes	Yes
Domestic Mutual Fund Investing in Foreign Stocks and Securities	No	No
Foreign Accounts and Foreign Non-Account Investment Assets Held by Foreign or Domestic Grantor Trust for Which You Are the Grantor	Yes, as to both foreign accounts and foreign non-account investment assets.	Yes, as to foreign accounts.

Table 23 — Continued

Foreign Assued Life Insurance or Annuity Contract with a Cash-Value	Yes	Yes
Foreign Hedge Funds and Foreign Private Equity Funds	Yes	No
Foreign Real Estate Held Directly	No	No
Foreign Real Estate Held through a Foreign Entity	No, but the foreign entity itself is a specified foreign financial asset and its maximum value includes the value of the real estate.	No
Foreign Currency Held Directly	No	No
Precious Metals Held Directly	No	No
Personal Property, Held Directly, Such as Art, Antiques, Jewelry, Cars and Other Collectibles	No	No
Social Security Type Program Benefits Provided by a Foreign Government	No	No

corporation is not operating an active business and the earnings are reported on Form 5471 and taxed each year, in the US.

2.2 If you own a Canadian trust

IRS Form 3520, Annual Return to Report Transactions with Foreign Trusts and Receipt of Certain Foreign Gifts, needs to be filed by US taxpayers if you are the owner of any part of a foreign trust, you received a distribution from a foreign trust, or received a gift or bequest of more than $100,000 from a foreign individual or foreign estate, or $15,671 (2016) for gifts received from a foreign (non-US) corporation or partnership. Again a general penalty of $10,000 may be assessed for late filing or non-filing. In addition, form 3520-A, Annual Information Return of a Foreign Trust With a US Owner is an annual information return of a foreign trust with a US owner and this form provides information about the foreign trust including an income statement and balance sheet of the foreign trust and an allocation of the income to the US owner. This form is prepared by the trustee or executor of the foreign trust. Penalties for not filing or late filing form 3520-A can be $10,000.

2.3 Registered Education Savings Plans

In Canada you can contribute to your child's or grandchild's postsecondary education by contributing to a Registered Education Savings Plan (RESP). With this type of plan, you or a grandparent can make non-tax-deductible contributions. You can make contributions up to a maximum of $50,000 per child. The Canadian government will provide a grant of 20% of the first $2,500 contributed per year ($500 per year), up to a lifetime maximum of $7,200 per child. Amounts in the RESP can be used for the child's after high school education and amounts are distributed to the student to pay for their education. The earnings are taxable to the student who would most likely not owe any tax because they would in a low or zero tax bracket. The beneficiary of the plan (i.e., the student) must have a Canadian Social Insurance Number. If the beneficiary does not attend a postsecondary education the RESP funds can be allocated to another child or can be contributed to your Registered Retirement Savings Plan (provided you have the RRSP room for the contribution). If the child does not attend postsecondary education the grant is lost.

Note: As long as the beneficiary maintains Canadian residency, the grant money can be used. If the beneficiary ceases to be a Canadian resident, the RESP can still be used, but the grant money has to be returned. A student attending university outside of Canada will typically continue to be considered a resident of Canada. If your child declares himself or herself a resident of a state in the US to obtain in-state tuition, the grant would be lost.

The income earned in the RESP is tax deferred and tax becomes payable on the income when the distribution is made to the student. Though the income is deferred in Canada, the income earned in the plan would be taxable in the US. It would also be considered a foreign trust and would require the preparation of Forms 3520 and 3520-A. A very simple solution to avoid these foreign reporting issues to the US would be for the owner of the RESP to not be a US person; such as spouse, sibling, grandparent or other relative or friend.

2.4 Tax-Free Savings Accounts

Canada allows you to contribute to a Tax-Free Savings Account (TFSA), similar to a Roth IRA. You can contribute up to $5,000 per year. No tax deduction is allowed for contributions to a TFSA, but the income earned in the TFSA accumulates tax free and withdrawals are tax free. If the maximum contribution is not made in the year, the amount can be carried forward so that if you did not make a $5,000 contribution last year you could make last year's contribution of $5,000 and this year's contribution of $5,000 in the current year. There is a 1% per month penalty for over contributions that exceed the maximum allowed.

Important: Even though the TFSA is tax free in Canada, the income earned in the TFSA is taxed in the US. Some US accountants have suggested that the TFSA is a foreign trust and therefore Forms 3520 and 3520-A would have to be prepared.

2.5 US entities

The use of Limited Liability Companies ("LLCs") in the US is very popular, but the LLC is not a good entity for use in Canada as it will lead to double tax. Canada views the LLC as a corporation, and any money paid out of the LLC is considered a dividend. Canadian income is recognized when the dividend is paid, which could be several years after the income is earned and taxed in the US. This timing difference will cause a problem when trying to use the foreign tax credit, resulting in double tax. As a Canadian resident, do not use LLCs.

Similarly, US taxpayers who have a corporation that has elected to be an S corporation have similar issues. An S corporation election can be made if all the shareholders are US persons. Canada does not recognize the S corporation as a flow-through entity and only distributions are treated as foreign investment income in Canada as a dividend. Therefore, if all the profits of the S corporation are distributed then there will not be double tax, however this does not typically happen as there always seems to be more profit than there is cash to pay a dividend.

There are other issues related to US corporations of Canadian residents. If the US corporation is deemed to be carrying on business in Canada then it will have to file a return in Canada. This would require it to file Form T2; a Canadian corporate tax return, and report its income and expenses from its Canadian activities. Carrying on business in Canada will depend if the corporation has a permanent establishment in Canada or not. It also depends on the level of activity in Canada. Carrying on business is also used to determine if the foreign corporation has to charge the sales tax.

2.6 Principal residence

Canada allows for an unlimited capital gain exemption from the sale of your personal residence. There are some limitations, such as when your home is part of a farm or ranch. You designate the property as your principal residence when you sell.

Americans owning a residence in Canada need to be aware that the US exemption is not unlimited and the definition of a principal residence is different. The US defines your residence as the place you called home at least two of the last five years. The US allows you to exempt gains up to $250,000 USD per person ($500,000 USD for a couple). Therefore, you could have a gain in the US even though the gain is exempt in Canada. If you retain your US home when you move to Canada, you have up to three years to sell the US home and still be able to declare it as your principal residence and take advantage of the capital gain exemption. After three years you would have no longer owned the home for at least two years out of the last five.

A possible planning opportunity would be that if only one spouse is an American, the residence could be bought by the non-American spouse.

2.7 Other issues

Americans in Canada should be aware that they can still deduct their mortgage interest and property taxes on their Canadian home on their US tax returns. However, principal residence mortgage interest and property taxes are not deductible on Canadian returns, unless claimed as part of an office in the home or self-employment. Taxpayers should be aware that in order to deduct expenses from employment for Canadian tax purposes they will require their employer to provide them with Form T2200, Declaration of Conditions of Employment.

Employers must certify on this Form T2200 that the employee is required, under the conditions of their employment, to have an office away from their place of business and to pay for supplies as well as car expenses that they are not reimbursed for during the course of employment.

In Canada, a principal residence is generally any residential property owned and occupied by you or your family at any time in the year. It can be a house, condominium, cottage, mobile home, motorhome, or live-aboard boat; essentially the criteria is that to be considered a residence, it must have dining, sleeping, and toilet facilities. A married or common-law couple can only have one principal residence at any one time.

3. Tax Planning Ideas

As a reminder, you want to reduce Canadian taxes so don't worry about US tax planning opportunities unless they also reduce your Canadian tax. Here are some of the more common Canadian tax planning ideas:

- Contribute as much as you can to an RRSP and contribute early in the year instead of waiting until the following February.

- Contribute up to $2,500 annually to a Registered Education Savings Plan (RESP) and earn a 20% government grant towards your children's education.

- If you have a spouse, combine your charitable donations and claim them on the higher-income spouse's return.

- If you own a business, consider incorporating and taking advantage of the potential benefit of tax deferral that a Canadian-Controlled Private Corporation provides.

- Contribute up to $5,500 annually to your TFSA for tax-sheltered growth.

- Moving assets to your spouse so that the income is earned and taxed to the spouse.

- The greatest tax planning idea is to exit Canada and make the US your home. This only requires that you spend at least 183 days a year in the US; see section 4. for more on this.

4. An Overview of the Tax Benefits of Moving to the US

Robert Keats describes in his book, *A Canadian's Best Tax Haven: The US*, how the US is a tax haven for Canadians. With 2016 tax increases, the tax differential between the US and Canada may be at its all-time high. Here are the main reasons that becoming a US resident is your best tax planning opportunity:

- US tax rates are generally much lower than in Canada.

- US tax brackets are much wider than the Canadian brackets. The highest Canadian federal tax bracket starts at $200,000 CAD, whereas the highest US tax bracket at $466,950 CAD or $648,542 CAD assuming the Canadian dollar stays in the $0.72 USD range.

- The difference between gross and taxable income is much greater in the US. This is because the US allows for more adjustments to gross income, primarily itemized deductions in which you can deduct things like home mortgage interest, state income tax, and property tax.

- The fact that Canada converts deductible expenses into credits using the lowest marginal tax rate of 15% reduces the benefit to you. The benefit of your deductions in the US is based on your marginal tax rate. So if you are in the 33% tax bracket, you will receive a benefit of $33 for every $100 of expense, whereas in Canada you would only receive $15 of benefit.

The rule of thumb before the 2016 tax increases was that a Canadian would save about a third on taxes by becoming a US resident. We would suspect that the savings will now be in the 35% to 40% range.

10

Canadian and US Death Taxes

Canada does not have an estate tax in the same manner that the US does, but it certainly has a death tax (although it is not called that). For most people, the taxes in Canada upon a death are much more far reaching than estate taxes in the US. For US citizens and green card holders, estate taxes are only a burden for very wealthy couples with estates worth in excess of $10.9 million USD ($5.45 million per person). Death taxes in Canada affect every Canadian taxpayer who owns capital property.

1. Canada's Death Tax: Deemed Disposition of Property

When a Canadian taxpayer dies, he or she is deemed to have disposed of all of his or her capital property as of the date of death. It is as if he or she sold the property for its fair market value immediately before he or she died. The difference between the deemed proceeds and the adjusted cost base of all of the taxpayer's capital property results in a net capital gain or loss that is reported on the taxpayer's final tax return. Depreciable capital property is similarly deemed to have been sold and often results in recapture of capital cost allowance or a terminal loss. If the deemed disposition results in a net capital loss, the loss can be carried back to apply against capital gains that were reported in the preceding three years before the taxpayer's death, or alternatively, if there are losses remaining, the loss can be used to offset other income on the final tax return or the return for the year prior to death.

If the taxpayer is married, then there can be a transfer of the capital property to the spouse, or a trust set up for the benefit of the spouse, as long as the spouse is a resident of Canada. This delays the disposition of property until the death of the surviving spouse. The deceased spouse's cost base is transferred over to the surviving spouse, unless there is a reason that should not happen, in which case an election can be made to transfer the property at the property's fair market value instead, which results in a capital gain but is useful when the deceased person has a capital gains deduction or a carried forward capital loss.

There are few deductions or exemptions from this capital gain. All rules that apply to actual capital gains from the sale of property also apply to deemed sales, such as the primary residence exemption. There is a deduction that can be claimed for dispositions or deemed dispositions of qualified Canadian farm property or fishing property that is transferred to a spouse, a child, or a grandchild. There is also an $824,176 CAD capital gain exemption for the disposition of qualified small-business corporation shares that can be used either during the taxpayer's lifetime or at the taxpayer's death when the shares are deemed sold.

Also, because Canada taxes its taxpayers on worldwide income, any capital property owned outside of Canada also is deemed sold at the taxpayer's death and included in the calculation of the deemed disposition resulting in net capital gain or loss. The death of the taxpayer could also result in death or estate taxes in the country where the property is located, the result of which is discussed later in this chapter.

A widely used technique used to offset the effect of the deemed disposition tax is to use an estate freeze which can be done when a resident owns a Canadian corporation. The technique issues common shares to the resident shareowner's children who takes back preferred shares, which allows the future growth in the firm to accrue to the children and freezes the parent's value of the shares at the value on the date of the transaction.

For someone who is considering moving to Canada, you will face the deemed disposition tax should you die as a Canadian taxpayer, on the appreciation in your assets from the date you enter Canada to the time of your death. The deemed disposition tax also applies if you ever decide to leave Canada to become a tax resident of another country (the "departure tax"). The deemed disposition of assets upon departure from Canada excludes certain assets such as Canadian registered retirement accounts and Canadian real property. The deemed disposition resulting from departure from Canada is reported on a taxpayer's final Canadian T1 (individual) tax return.

There is relief from departure tax for short-term residents. Short-term residents are generally individuals who move to Canada and are resident for less than five years. These individuals will not be subject to the departure tax rules. Also, someone who is resident in Canada for no more than 60 months in the 120 months preceding departure from Canada would not be subject to departure tax on property that was owned by the individual before becoming a Canadian resident, or that was acquired while a Canadian resident by bequest or inheritance.

Generally, a deemed disposition of a deceased person's capital assets are reported on his or her final T1 return. The due date for filing the return and to pay any tax owing depends on when the person died based on the following dates.

Period when death occurred	Due date for the final return
January 1 to October 31	April 30 of the following year
November 1 to December 31	Six months following the date of death

If the return is filed late and payment of any tax due has not been paid, there will be penalties and interest. The tax is due when the return is due. It is possible, however, to delay the payment of tax that results from a deemed disposition by filing Form T2057 — Election to Defer Payment of Income Tax, Under Subsection 159(5) of the *Income Tax Act* — by a Deceased Taxpayer's Legal Representative or Trustee. The tax can be deferred as long as there is security pledged for the payment of tax, and interest will be charged from the date the tax was originally due to the date it is paid.

2. Gift Tax in Canada

There is no gift tax in Canada. If you receive a gift or make a gift there will generally be no tax implications to the giver or the receiver. However, if the gift is made using capital (appreciable) property, you will have to compute the property's fair market value and pay tax on any capital gain. The person receiving the gift will now have the fair market value as of the date of the gift as their "cost" in the property given.

If money or capital property is given or loaned to a spouse or a related minor child, attribution rules will apply.

2.1 Attribution rules

If income-producing property, or money which is used to purchase income-producing property, is transferred or loaned to a related minor, either directly or indirectly, or by means of a trust, the income from the property will normally be attributed back to the person giving the gift or loan. The capital gains from the property will be considered capital gains of the minor. A related minor is a child who is under 18 years old and does not deal with the individual at arm's length, or is a niece or nephew of the individual.

If income-producing property, or money which is used to purchase income-producing property, is transferred or loaned to a spouse, either directly or indirectly, or by means of a trust, the income and capital gains from the property will normally be attributed back to the person giving the gift or loan.

In transfers to a related minor or to a spouse, any income earned from the original income (secondary income) will be considered income of the minor or spouse. An example would be where dividend-producing shares are transferred to a minor or spouse, and dividends are used to purchase more shares. The dividends from the additional shares would be income of the minor or spouse.

Note: The attribution rules apply only to property income, not to business income earned from money or business assets transferred. The attribution rules do not apply to loans where interest is charged at a rate at least equivalent to the specified rate of interest.

3. Probate in Canada

Although probate fees are not technically a tax, they can be a substantial estate expense. What are typically referred to as probate fees are actually court costs for the probate process for a deceased person's estate. Table 24 shows probate fees as of September 2015 by province.

In addition to the court probate costs, if you hire a lawyer there will be lawyer fees which are usually charged as a percentage of the estate and are approximately 2% or less, depending on the size of the estate.

4. US Death Taxes

You cannot escape US estate and gift taxes just by leaving the US! People who are still citizens of the United States will always be subject to the US transfer tax system; likewise they will always be subject to US income tax. The same thing applies to green card holders who have not surrendered their card and status as US Lawful Permanent Residents.

4.1 Estate tax issues for expatriated US citizens

Estate planning for US ex-pats can be very complicated, and as complicated as the issues are for income tax compliance, estate tax issues are a subset of a broader spectrum of estate planning concerns. Estate planning has to do with more than just estate taxes; we recommend that you work with an estate planning attorney who is well versed in the issues of international estate issues when developing your estate documents.

Table 24
COURT PROBATE COSTS

	Court Probate Costs
Alberta	$35 for estates under $10,000 $135 for estates between $10,000 and $24,999 $275 for estates between $25,000 and $124,999 $400 for estates between $125,000 and $249,999 $525 for estates of $250,000 or more
British Columbia	$0 for estates under $25,000 $6 for every $1,000 (or part of $1,000) that exceeds $25,000 but is less than $50,001 $14 for every $1,000 (or part of $1,000) that exceeds $50,000 There is also an administration fee of $208 for estate over $25,000.
Manitoba	$70 for estates $10,000 or less $7 for every $1,000 (or portion of $1,000) that exceeds $10,000
New Brunswick	$25 for estate $5,000 or less $50 for estates over $5,000, up to $10,000 $75 for estates over $10,000, up to $15,000 $100 for estate over $15,000, up to $20,000 $5 per $1,000 (or portion of $1,000) over $20,000
Newfoundland and Labrador	$60 for the first $1,000 $60 for estates over $1,000 on the first $1,000, plus $6 peer $100 (.6%) for estates over $1,000
Northwest Territories	$25 for estates $10,000 or less $100 for estates over $10,000, up to $25,000 $200 for estates over $25,000, up to $125,000 $300 for estates over $125,000, up to $250,000 $400 for estates over $250,000
Nova Scotia	$83.0 for estates $10,000 or less $208.98 for estates over $10,000, up to $25,000 $347.70 for estates over $25,000, up to $50,000 $973.45 for estates over $50,000, up to $100,000 $16.45 for every $1,000 (or portion of $1,000) that exceeds $100,000, plus $973.45 for the first $100,000
Nunavut	$25 for estates $10,000 or less $100 for estates over $10,000, up to $25,000 $200 for estates over $25,000, up to $125,000 $300 for estates over $125,000, up to $250,000 $400 for estates over $250,000

Table 24 — Continued

Ontario	$0 for estate of $1,000 or less $5 for every $1,000 (or portion of $1,000) for the first $50,000 Plus $15 for each $1,000 (or portion of $1,000) over $50,000
Prince Edward Island	$50 for estates $10,000 or less $100 for estates over $10,00, up to $25,000 $200 for estate over $25,000, up to $50,000 $400 for estate over $50,000, up to $100,000 $400 for estate over $100,000 ,plus $4 for every $1,000 (or portion of $1,000) over $100,000
Quebec	$105 for a natural person $118 for legal person
Saskatchewan	$7 for every $1,000 (or portion of $1,000) of the estate
Yukon	$0 for estates up to $25,000 (generally) $140 for estates that exceed $25,000

A basic issue is whether one country will consider your will to have been validly executed and respect the will as being valid. If a will is determined to be invalid, a US court, for instance, may not allow the will to be probated. Fortunately, the Convention Providing a Uniform Law on the Form of an International Will and The Hague Convention Relating to the Form of Testamentary Dispositions stipulate elements of the form of wills so that other jurisdictions will consider them to be valid. There are dual wills, which are particularly used when owning real property in a foreign country, but these can be problematic if they are not coordinated in a way that eliminates confusion as to which will prevails in the transfer of assets. In other words, if two wills are presented and both could be considered to be valid with respect to the transfer of a deceased person's asset, then the court may decide which one to use or, even worse, invalidate both wills.

The US has a system of taxation that is imposed on the gratuitous transfer of wealth from one person to another (gift tax) and from one generation to another (estate tax). This system is collectively called the federal tax system and is composed of three taxes:

- A gift tax that applies to transfers that occur during one's lifetime.

- An estate tax that applies to transfers after tax.

- A generation-skipping tax that can occur either during one's lifetime or after death and is applied when someone attempts to avoid the gift or estate tax at each generation.

As a US citizen who lives in Canada, you will have a full unified tax credit available which provides a $5.45 million USD (2016) exclusion amount from gift and estate taxes for you. If you are married and your spouse is also a US citizen, you can be assured that you will not have a US estate or gift tax until you have transferred over $10.9 million USD (two times the exclusion amount of $5.45 million USD) of your combined estate to your heirs. For US citizens, the amount of exclusion available to you is equal to your basic exclusion amount plus the unused exclusion of your US citizen spouse. The deceased spouse's unused exclusion is only available if an election is made on the deceased spouse's estate tax return, IRS Form 706 United States Estate (and Generation-Skipping Transfer) Tax Return, and the election can only be made if an estate tax return is filed. So you may want to file an estate tax return even if one is not required because the deceased spouse's estate was not large enough to owe tax.

The estate is calculated for US persons on their worldwide gross assets which include the following:

- Life insurance proceeds payable to your estate or, if you owned the policy, payable to your heirs.

- The value of certain annuities or pensions payable to your estate or your heirs.

- The value of certain property you transferred out of your estate within three years preceding the death.

Less allowable deductions, which include the following:

- Funeral expenses paid out of your estate.

- Debts you owed at the time of your death.

- The value of property passing to your spouse (this is known as the marital deduction and applies to transfers to citizens only).

- Charitable deductions made from your estate to a qualified charity (most Canadian charities qualify, but are subject to a limit).

4.2 Passing assets to a non-citizen spouse

A provision of the US federal Estate and Gift Tax laws allow the unrestricted transfer of assets to a US citizen spouse at any time, including at the death of the transferor, free from tax. This marital deduction is not permitted to a non-citizen spouse. If one spouse is not a US citizen, direct gifts and direct bequests by a deceased spouse to a noncitizen spouse do not qualify for a marital deduction. As part of this provision, gifts in trust that would otherwise qualify for a marital deduction will not qualify when the spouse is not a citizen. That is unless the trust meets certain requirements as a Qualified Domestic Trust (QDOT). A marital deduction is permitted if the property transfers to a QDOT.

A deceased spouse can leave assets to a surviving non-citizen spouse, estate-tax free, up to the decedent's estate tax exemption ($5.45 million USD in 2016). If a US citizen spouse's worldwide estate is greater than the exemption, properly drafted estate documents should include QDOT provisions. A QDOT is statutorily defined as a trust that permits married couples with at least one non-citizen spouse to take advantage of the marital deduction. The QDOT does not eliminate the US estate tax; it merely postpones the tax until the death of the surviving spouse or other subsequent taxable event. The postponed tax always remains that of the first decedent spouse. A surviving spouse's exclusion amount cannot be used to shelter QDOT assets from estate tax. Also, the QDOT tax remains equal to the tax that would have been imposed if the amount involved in the taxable event had been included in the first decedent's estate - at the tax rate that was in effect at the decedent's death. There are certain requirements that would have to be considered to form a QDOT for a nonresident of the US including:

- The QDOT must have at least one trustee who is an individual US citizen or a domestic US corporation.
- The executor of the estate must make an irrevocable QDOT election to qualify for the marital deduction on the deceased US citizen spouse's estate tax return (Form 706) within nine months from the date of death.

If the QDOT has assets of $2 million or less, then no more than 35% of the value can be in real property outside of the US or else —

- the US trustee must be a bank;
- the individual US trustee must furnish a bond for 65% of the value of the QDOT assets at the transferor's demise; or
- the individual US trustee must furnish an irrevocable letter of credit to the US government for 65% of the value.

If the QDOT has assets in excess of $2 million, then either —

- the US trustee must be a bank;
- the individual US trustee must furnish a bond for 65% of the value of the QDOT assets at the transferor's death; or
- the individual US trustee must furnish an irrevocable letter of credit to the US government for 65% of the value.

The primary difference between the unlimited marital deduction allowed to a US-citizen spouse and the unlimited deferral to a non-US citizen spouse using a QDOT is that assets passed to a US citizen can be consumed before death and never have to be included in the surviving spouse's estate. If that happened, there would be no tax due on those assets in the surviving spouse's estate. With a QDOT, however, there is no chance of that; any distributions of principal from a QDOT triggers an estate tax. The QDOT is designed to ensure that the property held in the trust will be charged US Federal estate tax, and the non-citizen spouse cannot avoid the tax that is due to the US. It only provides a deferral of that tax.

If the surviving spouse is the US citizen spouse, then there is no estate tax or transfer tax due. If the spouse is a citizen of the US, any gifts that you give to the US citizen spouse during your lifetime are free from US federal gift tax as well.

If the spouse is the non-citizen spouse, then the special tax-free treatment for lifetime gifts to non-citizen spouses is limited to $148,000 per year (in 2016). This amount is indexed for inflation. That is in addition to the exemption amount that can be either used during your lifetime or at your death; however, you should note that a gift tax return may be due in the US when transfers are made to your non-citizen spouse.

Caution: Be careful that you do not accidentally gift your non-US citizen spouse money that might exceed the annual limit. This might be accomplished by transferring separate or matrimonial property in to a joint account or jointly buying a home. If you come to the US and decide to cash out your RRSP and place the proceeds into a joint account, you will be making a gift that may exceed the annual limit.

4.3 Jointly held property

The rules surrounding jointly held property can be very complicated, and if you are a couple with a US citizen spouse and a non-citizen, you should seek advice from an estate planning attorney with cross-border experience. As an example, if a surviving spouse is not a US citizen but his or her deceased spouse was a US citizen, then 100% of the value of jointly held property is includable in the first decedent's estate for US estate tax purposes, except to the extent the executor can substantiate the contributions of the non-citizen spouse to the acquisition of the property. If the property is located in the US, then the surviving non-US citizen spouse could be subject to US estate taxes if he or she continues to hold the property until his or her demise (the US estate taxes for persons who are not US citizens, follows). For income tax purposes, the surviving spouse would generally receive the US property with a cost base equal to the market value of the deceased spouse's share of the property, so if the surviving spouse sells the property soon after receiving it, there would be no US income tax due. The determination of how US property passes to a surviving spouse and the percentage ownership of the property for which the cost base gets stepped up to the value as of the date of death depends on how the property is titled. For more details on how a Canadian can own US property and the tax (income and estate) consequences, we recommend that you read *Buying Real Estate in the US: The Concise Guide for Canadians*. However, keep in mind that if the deceased spouse was a Canadian resident, there would have been a deemed disposition that would have been reported on his or her final tax return, and the surviving spouse would receive the property at its fair market value as the cost basis for Canadian income tax purposes as well.

4.4 Issues for non-US persons (citizens or green card holders) who own US property

As complicated as the previous discussion was for US estate tax issues for US citizens who have expatriated, it is even more complicated for non-US citizens who own property in the US. An entire book could be devoted to the US transfer tax system and how it relates to US expatriates, green card holders, and nonresidents of the US owning US property. The matters that we are pointing out in this book merely brush the surface of the system of US estate and gift tax issues to help acquaint you to the complexities.

The Internal Revenue Code is similar to the *Income Tax Act* in Canada; it determines who is subject to transfer taxes using a different set of rules than is used for the income tax system. For tax purposes, there are US persons (residents or citizens) and nonresident aliens (nonresidents who are also non-citizens). For transfer tax purposes, there are three categories of individuals: US citizens, US domiciliaries which are resident aliens, and US non-domiciliaries, which are nonresident aliens.

A US green card holder is, by definition, a Lawful Permanent Resident of the US and is therefore taxed as a US resident until the green card is surrendered. This means that if you move to Canada as a green card holder, and you do not surrender your green card, you could continue to be subject to the income-, estate-, and gift-tax laws of the US.

If you are moving to Canada and either you or your spouse is not a US citizen, but you still plan to spend time in the US, you should be aware that the tests to determine tax residency for income tax purposes for a non-US citizen are somewhat different than the tests used to determine residency for transfer taxes. For transfer tax purposes, a concept of "domicile" becomes very important. Having domicile has nothing to do with the number of days you are present in the US. The number of days you are present in the US is the major test for residency, under the income tax rules. Domicile has to do with your intent. Your intent to live and stay in the US or elsewhere indefinitely determines domicile. The concept of domicile is very subjective, yet very important, because if you are deemed to be a US domiciliary, you will be subject to US estate taxes on your worldwide assets. It is possible to be a non-citizen for income tax purposes but be a US domiciliary for transfer tax purposes.

The IRS does not define the term "domicile" using objective standards. Instead, there are US Treasury (the IRS is an organization within the Department of the Treasury) regulations that provide a subjective set of tests based on one's intent to remain indefinitely in the US. The regulations use factors such as the following:

- The duration of stay in the US and other countries

- The frequency of travel between the US and other countries and between places abroad

- The size, cost, and nature of the individual's houses or other dwelling places and whether those places are owned or rented

- The area in which the houses or other dwelling places are located

- The location of expensive and cherished personal possessions

- The location of family and close friends

- The location of a person's church and club memberships and where he or she participates in community activities

- The location of any business interests

- Declarations of residence or intent made in visa or green card applications, wills, deeds, trusts, letters, and other documentation

- Motivations such as the avoidance of the miseries of war or political regression

- Visa status

4.5 Treaty

The Treaty provides some further guidance and can be used to supersede the IRS for determining domicile. It provides that residency for estate tax purposes (domicile) is determined using the same methodology as used under the Treaty, if the deceased taxpayer's estate is relying on the Treaty in calculating the tax. However, domicile may be desired because, as a US domiciliary, you would be entitled to the $5.45 million USD (per person) exclusion amount that is available to US citizens.

Canadians who are US non-domiciliaries and who own property in the US are subject to US estate tax on certain property deemed to be situated in the US. Under the Internal Revenue Code, the estate of a non-domiciliary, noncitizen of the US is subject to US estate tax only on specific US situs assets that collectively exceed $60,000 USD in value. Fortunately, the Treaty provides a two-part relief for this. The first relief is afforded through Paragraph 8, Article XXIX B, of the Treaty which provides that, for Canadians with gross estates of less than $1.2 million USD ($5.45 million USD for 2016), the tax will only be on the gains of real property situated in the US and personal property that forms a part of a US business. The second relief comes from Paragraph 2 of Article XXIX B which grants a pro-rata unified credit to the estate of a Canadian resident decedent for purposes of computing US estate tax. The allowed pro-rata credit is determined by multiplying the US exemption by a fraction, the numerator of which is the value of the part of the gross estate situated in the US and the denominator of which is the value of the entire gross estate wherever situated.

In other words, a nonresident can generally have up to $60,000 of US assets before he or she would be subject to US estate taxes. However, the Treaty can be used to increase the $60,000 exemption by providing Canadians who are nonresidents and non-citizens of the US with a proportionate allocation of the $5.45 million USD exemption allowed to US citizens and domiciliaries. The exemption can never be less than the $60,000, so for smaller estates, a person can use the $60,000 USD exemption allowed under the Internal Revenue Code. For larger estates, a Canadian nonresident of the US can use the Treaty formula of US assets divided by worldwide assets, times $5.45 million USD.

For example, a Canadian resident who is not a US citizen and is not a resident of the US owns a condo in Arizona worth $250,000 USD. That person has a worldwide net worth, including life insurance, of $1,500,000 USD. That means that 17 percent of the person's assets are in the US and he or she can use 17 percent of the $5,450,000 exemption, or $926,500. Since the exemption ($926,500) is greater than the amount of assets in the US ($250,000), there is no US estate tax.

Note: The estate of the person in the example above would have to file an estate tax return even though there is no estate tax due. Believe it or not the IRS does not trust you, you must file a return and prove to them the numbers you are claiming on the estate tax return. This is done using receipts, appraisals, etc.

Since the Treaty allowed for the extra exclusion, not a US tax law, an estate tax return must be filed to make an election to invoke the Treaty provision. Without the benefit of the Treaty, the exemption would have been limited to $60,000. However, if the value of the US assets was equal to or less than $60,000, no return would have to be filed.

How do you determine what constitutes US assets, also known as US "situs property"? The rules for determining US situs property for a nonresident, non-US citizen are determined under the laws of the Internal Revenue Code; the treaty does not provide guidance in determining US situs property. US situs property includes personal property normally located in the US and includes such things as vehicles, jewelry, artwork, boats, RVs, furniture, and collectibles. Shares of US corporations, regardless of where they were purchased or where they are physically held and certain bonds and notes issued by US residents and corporations are also included, even if those securities are held in Canadian registered accounts. This includes shares of mutual funds and electronically traded funds (ETFs) issued by US companies. It does not include American Depository Receipts (ADRs) of foreign corporations, which are shares of foreign corporations listed on a US stock exchange. It includes interests in certain trusts if the assets in the trust have US situs. It also includes any business-related assets owned by a sole proprietor and used in a US business. Bequests to charitable organizations in the US reduce US situs property.

Assets normally excluded from the numerator of the formula used for a nonresident include US bank deposits, proceeds of life insurance on the life of the decedent, and shares or notes of non-US corporations. In general, if interest from a debt instrument to a nonresident of the US is exempt from US taxation, the underlying debt obligation is likely to be excluded from the US estate.

Neither the US income tax code nor the regulations specifically address the situs (legal location) of partnership interests for estate tax purposes, and case law and rulings are inconclusive. It is reasonable to conclude that a nonresident alien's interest in a US partnership, particularly if it is engaged in a US trade or business, will be included as US situs property.

Deductions for expenses and debts of a nonresident's US estate are allowed, but only in proportion to the value of the US estate to the worldwide estate. For example, if the deceased nonresident has an outstanding loan for $30,000, and the US estate (not including the deduction for the loan) is $500,000 and is part of a worldwide estate of $1,000,000, then 50 percent of the loan would be deducted from the US estate. There is, in effect, an exception for real property encumbered by nonrecourse indebtedness. Because the debt is nonrecourse, if the real property is included in the US estate, then the entire indebtedness can be deducted.

All of the US estate property is combined, net of deductions, and is used as the numerator in the estate tax calculation for a nonresident Canadian in the US.

The denominator is the US non-citizen non-domiciliary's worldwide estate (or the "gross estate"). The IRS sets the rules for determining what is included in the nonresident's worldwide state. The IRS defines the gross estate of a decedent as including "all property, real or personal, tangible or intangible, wherever situated." It includes all of the assets that were used in the numerator of the formula, and it also includes interests in corporation, life insurance proceeds, and bank deposits including checking, savings, money market accounts, Guaranteed Investment Certificates (GICs), and Certificates of Deposit (CDs).

It includes the full value of Canadian-controlled private corporations which you control or have controlled and in which you still own shares, and the present value of all future payments you might leave to a spouse under the spousal benefit of your pension plan.

All investment accounts and stocks and bonds owned in certificate form are included. Retirement accounts are included, such as US Individual Retirement Accounts (IRAs) and 401(k)s. It includes Canadian mutual funds, Canadian Registered Retirement Savings Plans, and Exchange-Traded Funds (ETFs).

Funeral expenses, administration expenses, debts, and claims against the estate are fully deductible from the gross estate. If property is located in a state that has a state death tax, there is also an allowable deduction for any state taxes that you may incur from the federal gross estate. Charitable deductions are made to either Canadian charities or US charities are deductible from the gross estate.

If property is being transferred to a spouse, a special elective "marital credit" is allowed by paragraph 3 of Article XXIX B of the Treaty for the deceased Canadian's estate who is filing the US estate tax return. The credit provides that the property transferred to a spouse who is a US or Canadian resident or a citizen of the US will be credited against the deceased spouse's gross estate (the denominator) and the US estate (the numerator). The credit that is allowed is the lesser of the unified tax credit that results from having a $5.45 million exemption (2016) and the US estate tax that would otherwise be imposed on the property. Thus, for most married Canadians who own property in the US, an estate tax would not become due until the death of the second spouse.

The Treaty provides relief to a double taxation issue that, not so long ago, had been problematic for Canadians and US persons who owned property in both countries, or for US citizens who would be subject to taxes resulting from both the deemed disposition of capital property in Canada and the US estate tax.

For a nonresident, non-citizen of the US who owns property that is subject to US estate taxes or has a taxable US estate given the rules described in this chapter, any taxes incurred in the US either for US federal or state estate or inheritance taxes may be credited toward taxes paid in Canada on the same property for capital gains resulting from the deemed disposition that occurs upon death. In other words, a foreign tax credit may be claimed against Canadian income tax for estate taxes paid in the US on the deceased's final Canadian tax return.

For a citizen of the US who is subject to both US estate taxes and taxes resulting from a deemed disposition in Canada, a credit can be taken either on the final Canadian tax return for the estate taxes paid in the US or on the US estate tax return (Form 706) for the taxes paid as a result of the deemed disposition of property in Canada.

5. US Foreign Trust Rules

In general, if you are the owner of a foreign trust, you are taxed on the income of that trust. A US person is treated as the owner of a foreign trust under the grantor trust rules which include someone who transfers assets to a foreign trust which has a US beneficiary of any portion of the trust. Each US owner must receive an Annual Information Return of Foreign Trust with a U.S. Owner (IRS Form 3520-A, page 3), which includes information about the foreign trust income he or she must report.

If you transfer appreciated assets to a non-grantor foreign trust, you are required to recognize the gain on transfers of those assets to the trust.

The thing to remember is that a great many trusts and/or their beneficiaries pay more tax than is necessary because they run afoul of the foreign trust rules. Whenever a trust is not entirely Canadian or completely US, meaning the grantor, the beneficiaries, and the trustee are all one or the other, you will most likely have unnecessary tax and reporting issues.

Example: If your parents who are not US persons (citizens, residents, or green card holders), form a Canadian trust and name you (a US person) as a beneficiary, they now have a US grantor trust and there are US tax and reporting issues that need to be addressed.

Caution: It should be clear to you by now that the international estate tax rules should not be taken lightly. It is essential when dealing with an estate with both US and Canadian property, or with US citizens who have expatriated, to seek professional advice from an expert in this field. We covered the basics of the death tax implications, but our discussion merely brushed the surface of the issues that could be encountered in a multinational estate. Furthermore, more than just tax implications need to be considered such as estate, trust, and probate laws that must be adhered to for the proper administration of an estate, and implications from the proper or improper titling of property. The international estate tax waters are deep and treacherous.

11

Tax for Americans Living in Canada

The US imposes a tax on worldwide income for individuals who are either US citizens or residents. If you are a US citizen or resident, you are also subject to US estate and gift tax laws, based on your worldwide assets.

Individuals that are generally subject to US tax are:

- US citizens
- Lawful Permanent Residents (green card holders)
- Those who meet the substantial presence test
- Those with income from US sources

We frequently get inquiries asking whether if a person owns a home or rental property in the US he or she will be subject to tax on worldwide income, or if he or she dies, will US estate tax be owed on their worldwide assets. If you are a not a citizen or resident of the US, your world income or assets WILL NOT be subject to US tax; you will only be subject to US income tax on your US income and US estate tax on your US assets. We go into more detail in the sections below.

1. US Citizens

There are two general ways to obtain citizenship through US citizen parents: one at birth, and one after birth but before the age of 18. The term "parents" includes the genetic father, the genetic mother, and the non-genetic gestational mother, if she is the legal parent at the time of birth under the law of the relevant jurisdiction. See Chapter 12 for a more complete explanation of how a person might be a US citizen and not know it.

2. Green Card Holders

The official name of a green card holder is Lawful Permanent Resident, and as such, you will typically be considered a US resident until the green card is surrendered. As a resident of the US, you are required to report your worldwide income on IRS form 1040. Because you will be considered a resident of the US even while living in Canada, you will have dual residency and from a US perspective, be known as a dual-status taxpayer. However, the Treaty has tie-breaker rules that can limit some of your tax reporting requirements. See below for a discussion of how the Treaty affects green card holders.

Important: The US immigration and income tax laws are not congruent and therefore if you are out of the country for more than six months a year, you could lose your residency status. However, this is from an immigration point of view only; the IRS will continue to consider you a resident for income tax purposes.

2.1 The Treaty as it applies to green card holders

If you are not a US citizen (alien), you are classified as a resident of the US in any calendar year you if you are a Lawful Permanent Resident of the United States at any time during such calendar year (green card holder), meet the substantial presence test, or make the first-year election on the tax return.

As a Canadian resident and green card holder, you are considered a "dual resident taxpayer." The Treaty has tie-breaker rules that apply to determine the residence (for purposes of the treaty) of an individual who otherwise would be treated as a resident of both the US and Canada. If as a green card holder, you are considered a resident of Canada under a tie-breaker rule, you may claim a treaty benefit as a nonresident alien for purposes of computing your US income tax liability with respect to that portion of the taxable year you were considered to be a dual resident taxpayer. A dual resident green card holder may compute his or her US income tax liability as if he or she were a nonresident alien by filing a Form 1040NR with a Form 8833 attached. If the tie-breaker rules do not provide a clear answer as to your residency, the competent authorities will have to decide, which means that you will have to write to the government and ask for a ruling.

2.2 Termination of green card status

You are a Lawful Permanent Resident (green card holder) if you have the status of having been lawfully accorded the privilege of residing permanently in the United States and such status has not been revoked by an administrative or judicial proceeding abandonment. In other words, green card holders continue to be US residents for tax purposes until their Lawful Permanent Resident status is rescinded or administratively or judicially determined to have been abandoned; merely leaving the US with no intention to return is not sufficient.

2.3 Expatriation

A long-term resident is an individual who had a green card in at least 8 of the previous 15 taxable years, ending with the taxable year during which the individual ceased to be a green card holder. You are not treated as a green card holder for any taxable year if you are treated as a resident of Canada for the taxable year under the provisions of the Treaty and you do not waive the benefits of such treaty applicable to residents of Canada.

If you ceased to be treated as a green card holder prior to February 6, 1995, you are not subject to the expatriation rules even if you would have been a long-term resident under the definition. In addition, if you ceased to be treated as a green card holder after February 5, 1995, and before June 17, 2008, but were not a long-term resident you are not subject to the expatriation rules.

There is an "exit tax" on certain individuals who cease to be treated as US citizens or long-term residents (expatriate) on or after June 17, 2008. Therefore, if you are considered a covered expatriate, you will be subject to an exit tax similar to Canada's deemed disposition tax. See below for details.

3. Surrendering Your Green Card

To surrender your lawful permanent residence status (green card), you must submit US State Department Form I-407 — Record of Abandonment of Lawful Permanent Residence Status.

There is no need to advise anyone before you leave the United States. After leaving, however, you should file the Form I-407 at the US embassy or consulate. Whether you submit Form I-407 in person or by mail, you must turn in your green card at the same time.

After you file, you will be interviewed by a US consular officer who will confirm that your abandonment of your green card is voluntary and that you understand the consequences of the abandonment. You will receive a copy of the Form I-407 as evidence of the abandonment of your Lawful Permanent Resident status. After you have abandoned your green card, we recommend that you keep a copy of the completed I-407 with your passport, when traveling to the United States, to avoid confusion as to your status.

3.1 Long-term residents of the US

If you were a Lawful Permanent Resident (green card holder) of the US for at least 8 of the last 15 years prior to giving up your permanent resident status, you must also take formal steps to advise the IRS of your relinquishment of residency. This involves filing a completed IRS Form 8854 — Initial and Annual Expatriation Statement, with the IRS.

As a long-term resident, you would terminate residency on the earliest of the following dates:

1. The date you voluntarily abandoned your Lawful Permanent Resident status by filing the Form I-407 with a US consular or immigration officer and they have determined that you have in fact, abandoned your Lawful Permanent Resident status.

2. The date you became subject to a final administrative order for your removal from the US under the Immigration and Nationality Act, and you have actually left the US as a result of that order.

3. If you were a dual resident of the US and a country with which the US has an income tax treaty (such as Canada), the date you commenced to be treated as a resident of that country and you determined that, for purposes of the treaty, you were a resident of the treaty country and gave notice to the Secretary of the Treasury of such treatment.

Even if you expatriate and are considered a nonresident alien, you may be classified as a "covered expatriate," which would subject you to an exit tax, similar to the tax Canada imposes on its residents when they leave Canada and become residents of another country. The exit tax imposes an immediate tax, as well as potential future taxes on the expatriate. A covered expatriate is either a US citizen or long-term resident who abandons or loses his or her status as a US citizen or permanent resident, and as of the day before expatriation has —

- average net income tax for the last five years of more than $161,000 (2016),

- net worth on the date of expatriation of $2,000,000 or more, or

- you fail to certify, under penalty of perjury, that you have complied with all US federal tax obligations for the five years preceding the date of your expatriation or termination of residency. Certification is done using Form 8854 (more on this form later). This form is completed when filing Form 1040 (or 1040NR) for the year of expatriation.

The income tax amount of $161,000 USD is increased for cost-of-living adjustment each year. There is no cost-of-living adjustment for the net worth amount of $2 million USD.

Note that the $161,000 amount is the tax, not the income. This means that if you assume an average or effective tax rate of 30%, you need to have an average taxable income of more than $535,000 (not gross income) for the last five years. This seems like a much higher threshold than $2 million USD net worth, so the vast majority of those expatriating will be considered a covered expatriate due to having a net worth in excess of $2 million.

If you expatriate and you are considered a covered expatriate, you will be subject to a "mark-to-market tax," also known as a deemed disposition of your worldwide assets. The mark-to-market tax requires that you recognize gain on assets as if they were sold at their fair market value on the day prior to your expatriation.

If you are a long-term resident, you have the option of using the fair market value of your assets on the day your US residency began. For the assets you owned when you moved to the US, this will, in most cases, be a higher number and therefore produce a lower gain than using the original purchase price.

There are three groups of assets that are not subject to the mark-to-market tax, but will be taxed using a different method: deferred compensation, tax-deferred accounts, and an interest in a non-grantor trust. If you have one or more of these types of accounts, you must file IRS Form W-8CE — Notice of Expatriation and Waiver of Treaty Benefits, within 30 days of expatriation. A non-grantor trust is irrevocable, where the grantor has given up all right, title, and interest in the principal of the trust. Only the trustee may revoke or terminate the trust. In a non-grantor trust, the grantor cannot be named as a trustee or beneficiary.

Deferred compensation is divided into two types, one that has a US payor that is required to withhold on all payments, and one for all other deferred compensation arrangements. Where US withholding is required, payment can be deferred until payment is made, but the withholding must be 30%. Though the Canada-US Treaty rate is 15% on pensions and annuities, the covered expatriate cannot use the Treaty to reduce the withholding. For all other deferred compensation arrangements, the accrued benefit will be treated as being received the day before expatriation.

Examples of deferred compensation plans include, a company pension or profit sharing plan (including 401(k) and 403(b) accounts), simplified employee pensions (SEP), and simplified retirement accounts (SIMPLE plans).

Important: Any interests in foreign pensions or retirement accounts are considered deferred compensation plans and are included in the expatriation tax. This includes your RRSPs, RRIFs, LIRAs, any Canadian company pension, government or military pension, but does not include Canadian Pension Plan, Quebec Pension Plan or Old Age Security, which are forms of social security.

Examples of tax-deferred accounts are individual retirement accounts (IRAs), qualified tuition plans (aka Section 529 Plans), Coverdell education savings accounts, health savings accounts, and an Archer Medical Savings Accounts (aka Archer MSAs). However, SEP and SIMPLE plans are treated as deferred compensation items described above. These plans are treated as if the entire interest was paid out on the day prior to expatriation.

A non-grantor trust is when the grantor gives the control of the trust property to a trustee other than themselves. In other words, a non-grantor trust is a trust that someone established for the benefit of someone other than themselves. So, if someone (your parents for example) established a trust in which you are the beneficiary, or at least one of the beneficiaries, the value of your share of the trust is subject to the expatriation tax. If you are the beneficiary of such a trust, the trustee must withhold 30% of any direct or indirect distributions. This withholding rule applies to both domestic (US) and foreign (non-US) trusts.

If you are subject to the expatriate tax regime, the US provides a capital gain exemption of $693,000 USD (2016 and indexed for inflation). This means that many of you will not owe tax upon expatriating. If your gain is greater than $693,000, you pay tax on the difference. If you are married and you are both long-term residents that are expatriating, you each have an exemption of $693,000. An important distinction is that a couple does not get $1,386,000 to split between them, they each get $693,000.

Example: If a couple had total gains of $1,300,000, which were evenly split between them, they would each have $650,000 of gains that would be fully exempt. However, if one spouse had $1,000,000 of gains and the other had $300,000 of gains, only $993,000 of gains would be exempt and tax would have to be paid on the other $307,000. One spouse would receive the full $693,000 of exemption and the other spouse would be able to exempt all $300,000 of their gains, for a total of $993,000.

Note: You can make an irrevocable election to defer the payment of the tax. If you make the election, the following rules apply:

1. You must make the election on a property-by-property basis.

2. The deferred tax on a particular property is due on the return for the tax year in which you dispose of the property.

3. Interest is charged for the period the tax is deferred.

4. The due date for the payment of the deferred tax cannot be extended beyond the earlier of the following dates.

   a. The due date of the return required for the year of death.

   b. The time that the security provided for the property fails to be adequate (see 5 below).

5. You must provide adequate security, such as a bond.

6. You must make an irrevocable waiver of any right under any treaty of the US that would preclude assessment or collection of any tax imposed under this expatriation regime.

7. You must file Form 8854 annually for each year, up to and including the year in which the full amount of deferred tax and interest is paid.

Once you abandon your Lawful Permanent Resident status, you permanently lose all privileges associated with a US green card; you can't simply change your mind later and get your green card back. You will not be able to enter, live in, or work anywhere in the US without getting a new entry visa or reapplying for a green card.

However, abandonment of your Lawful Permanent Resident status does not bar you from applying for Lawful Permanent Resident status in the future.

4. Substantial Presence Test

This section applies to Canadians who are not US citizens or green card holders. We talk about this issue because many Americans living in Canada are married to Canadians who are not US citizens or green card holders.

You will be considered a US resident for tax purposes if you meet the substantial presence test for the calendar year. To meet this test, you must be physically present in the United States on at least:

1. 31 days during the current year, and

2. 183 days during the three-year period that includes the current year and the two years immediately before that, counting:

   - all the days you were present in the current year, and

   - $1/3$ of the days you were present in the first year before the current year, and

   - $1/6$ of the days you were present in the second year before the current year.

   You were physically present in the United States on 120 days in each of the years 2014, 2015, and 2016. To determine if you meet the substantial presence test for 2015, count the full 120 days of presence in 2016, 40 days in 2015 ($1/3$ of 120), and 20 days in 2014 ($1/6$ of 120). Since the total for the 3-year period is 180 days, you are not considered a resident under the substantial presence test for 2016. The formula for spending 121 days each year in the US would result in 181 days and 122 days each year would result in 183 days. This is sometimes referred to as the 120-day rule. If you are in the US year after year for 120 days or less, you will not be considered a US resident. If you fail part two of the test (formula test), you need to file Form 8840 to avoid being considered a US resident and being taxed on your worldwide income.

Caution: Any part of a day counts as a day in the US. In addition to including the days you arrive and leave the US, it includes days you come across the border to shop or buy gasoline. A layover in a US airport to catch a connecting flight does not count as a day in the US While you technically will not need to file Form 8840 if the formula results in less than 183 days, we recommend that if you are within a few days of 183, that you do file to be safe; you may have missed a day or counted wrong.

4.1 Days of presence in the US

You are treated as present in the US on any day you are physically present in the country, at any time during the day. However, there are exceptions to this rule. Do not count the following as days of presence in the US for the substantial presence test:

- Days you commute to work in the US from a residence in Canada, if you regularly commute from Canada

- Days you are in the US for less than 24 hours, when you are in transit between two places outside the US

- Days you are in the US as a crew member of a foreign vessel

- Days you are unable to leave the US because of a medical condition that develops while you are in the US

- Days you are an exempt individual

4.2 Exempt individual

Do not count days for which you are an exempt individual. The term "exempt individual" does not refer to someone exempt from US tax, but to anyone in the following categories who is exempt from counting days of presence in the US:

- An individual temporarily present in the United States as a foreign government-related individual

- A teacher or trainee temporarily present in the United States under a J or Q visa, who substantially complies with the requirements of the visa

- A student temporarily present in the United States under an F, J, M, or Q visa, who substantially complies with the requirements of the visa

- A professional athlete temporarily in the United States to compete in a charitable sports event.

If you exclude days of presence in the United States because you fall into a special category, you must file a fully-completed Form 8843 — Statement for Exempt Individuals and Individuals with a Medical Condition.

4.3 Closer connection exception

Even if you passed the substantial presence test you can still be treated as a nonresident alien if you qualify for the closer connection exception. As long as you were not in the US more than 182 days in the year and you only failed the test due to the formula, you can file Form 8840 — Closer Connection Exception Statement for Aliens.

5. Residency Starting and Ending Dates

An alien's period of residency in the United States must have an official starting date and ending date. The rules for determining these dates are as follows in the next sections.

5.1 Starting date under the green card test

If you meet the green card test at any time during a calendar year, but do not meet the substantial presence test for that year, your residency starting date is the first day in the calendar year on which you are present in the US as a Lawful Permanent Resident. This is the date on which the United States Citizenship and Immigration Services (USCIS) has officially approved your petition to become an immigrant.

If you receive your green card while abroad, then the residency starting date is your first day of physical presence in the United States after you receive your green card. The Internal Revenue Code allows you to be treated as a resident alien for the entire calendar year if you were a Lawful Permanent Resident of the United States at any time during the calendar year, if you have been present in the United States for at least one day during the calendar year. You will typically want to make the election to be treated as a US resident for the entire year on your initial US tax return.

If you were a US resident during any part of the preceding calendar year and you are a US resident for any part of the current year, you will be considered a US resident at the beginning of the current year.

If you meet both the green card test and the substantial presence test in the same year, your residency starting date is the earlier of:

- the first day you are present in the United States during the year you pass the substantial presence test, or

- the first day you are present in the US as a Lawful Permanent Resident (green card holder).

If, at the end of your tax year, you are married and one spouse is a US citizen or a resident alien and the other is a nonresident alien, you can choose to treat the nonresident as a US resident. This includes situations in which one of you is a nonresident alien at the beginning of the tax year, but a resident alien at the end of the year, and the other is a nonresident alien at the end of the year. You will typically want to make this election to file as if both spouses were full-year residents of the US. You are probably thinking that this does not make sense; why would anyone want to report more income to the US than is required? The reasons reporting both spouses' income for the entire year typically makes sense are that the ability to file jointly allows you more deductions against your income, and that the foreign tax credit will typically offset any US tax.

Hint: File your return with and without the elections to be treated as a full-year resident and having both spouses treated as full-year residents. You will typically find that making the elections is beneficial.

5.2 Starting date under the substantial presence test

If you meet the substantial presence test for a calendar year, your residency starting date is generally the first day you are present in the US during that calendar year.

If you were a US resident during any part of the preceding calendar year and you are a US resident for any part of the current year, you will be considered a US resident at the beginning of the current year.

If you meet both the green card test and the substantial presence test in the same year, your residency starting date is the earlier of:

- the first day you are present in the United States during the year you pass the substantial presence test, or

- the first day you are present in the US as a Lawful Permanent Resident (green card holder).

Note: An exempt individual under the substantial presence test is not considered to be present in the US during the exempt individual period for purposes of determining the residency starting date under the substantial presence test. This rule may result in situations in which the residency starting date for an exempt individual under the substantial presence test is later than when the exempt individual arrived in the US.

If, at the end of your tax year, you are married and one spouse is a US citizen or a resident alien and the other is a nonresident alien, you can choose to treat the nonresident as a US resident. This includes situations in which one of you is a nonresident alien at the beginning of the tax year, but a resident alien at the end of the year, and the other is a nonresident alien at the end of the year.

5.3 Starting date under the first-year choice

If you do not meet either the green card test or the substantial presence test for the current year (for example, 2015) or the prior year (2014), and you did not choose to be treated as a US resident for part of the prior year (2014), but you meet the substantial presence test in the following year (2016), you can choose to be treated as a US resident for part of the current year (2015). To make this first-year choice, you must:

1. Be present in the US for at least 31 days in a row in the current year, and

2. Be present in the US for at least 75% of the number of days beginning with the first day of the 31-day period and ending with the last day of the current year. (For purposes of this 75% requirement, you can treat up to five days of absence from the US as days of presence in the US.)

If you make the first-year choice, your residency starting date for the current year is the first day of the earliest 31-day period that you use to qualify for the choice. You are then treated as a US resident for the rest of the year.

If you are present for more than one 31-day period and you satisfy condition above for each of those periods, your residency starting date is the first day of the first 31-day period. If you are present for more than one 31-day period but you satisfy condition above only for a later 31-day period, your residency starting date is the first day of the later 31-day period.

Example: Jason is a citizen of Canada. He came to the US for the first time on November 1, 2014, and was there on 31 consecutive days (from November 1 through December 1, 2014). Jason returned to Canada on December 1 and returned to the US on December 17, 2012. He stayed in the US for the rest of the year. During 2015, Jason was a resident of the US under the substantial presence test. Jason can make the first-year choice for 2014 because he was in the US in 2014 for a period of 31 days in a row (November 1 through December 1) and for at least 75% of the days following (and including) the first day of his 31-day period (46 total days of presence in the US divided by 61 days in the period from November 1 through December 31 equals 75.4%). If Jason makes the first-year choice, his residency starting date will be November 1, 2014.

You must attach a statement to Form 1040 (make an election) to make the first-year choice for the current year. The statement must contain your name and address and specify the following:

- That you are making the first-year choice for the current year.

- That you were not a US resident in the prior year.

- That you are a US resident under the substantial presence test in the following year.

- The number of days of presence in the US during the following year.

- The date or dates of your 31-day period of presence and the period of continuous presence in the US during the current year.

- The date or dates of absence from the US during the current year (that you are treating as days of presence under the first-year choice).

You cannot file Form 1040 or the statement until you meet the substantial presence test in the following year. If you have not met the test for the following year as of April 15 of that year, you can request an extension of time for filing your Form 1040 until a reasonable period after you have met that test. To request an extension to file until October 15 of the following year, use Form 4868, Application for Automatic Extension of Time to File US Individual Income Tax Return.

Important: Once you make the first-year choice, you may not revoke it without the approval of the Internal Revenue Service.

If you do not follow the procedures discussed here for making the first-year choice, you will be treated as a nonresident alien for all of 2014. However, this does not apply if you can show by clear and convincing evidence that you took reasonable actions to become aware of the filing procedures and significant steps to comply with the procedures.

5.4 Starting date under the terms of the treaty

In general, your residency starting date under the terms of the Treaty is the date on which you first satisfy the definition of a resident under the terms of the Treaty. As a general rule, the Treaty looks first to the domestic tax law of each country to define residency for that country. If dual residency in two countries results, then the Treaty provides tie-breaker rules to determine to which country residency pertains.

5.5 Residency during the next year

If you are a US resident during any part of the following year and you are a resident during any part of the current year, you will be taxed as a resident through the end of the current year. This applies whether you have a closer connection to a foreign country during the current year, whether you are a US resident under the substantial presence test, or whether you are a US resident under the green card test.

5.6 Ending date under the green card test

Your last day of presence in the US on which you are considered to be a Lawful Permanent Resident of the US is the residency ending date under the immigration laws of the US.

However, green card holders who reside outside the US are still considered to be resident aliens of the US for tax purposes, unless such persons: (1) voluntarily turn in their green cards to USCIS and renounce their US immigrant status; (2) have their immigrant status administratively revoked by USCIS; or (3) have their immigrant status judicially revoked by a US federal court.

Caution: A Lawful Permanent Resident (green card holder) for at least 8 of the last 15 years who ceases to be a US Lawful Permanent Resident may be subject to special reporting requirements and tax provisions.

5.7 Ending date under the substantial presence test

In general, if you meet the substantial presence test, your residency ending date is your last day of presence in the US followed by a period during which:

1. You are not present in the United States,

2. You have a closer connection to a foreign country than to the US, and

3. You are not a resident of the US during the calendar year following that of your last day of presence in the US.

Under the general rule, the residency ending date is December 31 of the calendar year in which you left the US.

However, an exception is allowed for a residency ending date earlier than December 31 in the alien's last calendar year in the US Under this exception the alien's residency ending date shall be the last day during the calendar year that the individual is physically present in the United States if, for the remainder of the calendar year:

- your tax home is in a foreign country, and

- you maintain a closer connection to that foreign country than to the US.

Note: An exempt individual is not considered to be present in the US during the exempt individual period for purposes of determining the residency ending date under the substantial presence test. This rule may result in situations in which a person who was once a resident under the substantial presence test and who later becomes an exempt individual, can become a nonresident alien once more without ever having left the US.

5.8 Statement required to establish your residency termination date

You must file a statement with the IRS to establish your residency termination date. You must sign and date this statement and include a declaration made under penalties of perjury.

The statement must be attached to your income tax return. If you are not required to file an income tax return, send the statement to the Department of the Treasury, Internal Revenue Service, Austin, Texas 73301-0215, on or before the due date for filing your income tax return.

The statement must contain the following information (as applicable):

1. Your name, address, US taxpayer identification number (if any), and US visa type and number (if any).

2. Your passport number and the name of the country that issued your passport.

3. The tax year for which the statement applies.

4. The last day that you were present in the US during the year.

5. Sufficient facts to establish you have maintained your tax home in and that you have a closer connection to a foreign country following your last day of presence in the US during the year or following the abandonment or rescission of your status as a Lawful Permanent Resident during the year.

6. The date that your status as a Lawful Permanent Resident was abandoned or rescinded.

7. Sufficient facts (including copies of relevant documents) to establish that your status as a Lawful Permanent Resident has been abandoned or rescinded.

8. If you can exclude days under the *de minimis* presence rule, include the dates of the days you are excluding and sufficient facts to establish that you have maintained your tax home in, and that you have a closer connection to, a foreign country during the period you are excluding.

6. Foreign-Earned Income Tax Exclusion

As a US citizen or green card holder, you will continue to have the same US tax filing requirements, as if you were still in the US. If you work as an employee or if you are self-employed, you will have "earned" income. The US allows you to exclude your foreign (non-US) income, up to $101,300 USD (2016) and your foreign housing exclusion, which is generally limited to 30%

of the income exclusion, or $30,390 USD ($83.26 per day) for 2016. A number of cities in Canada qualify for a higher daily dollar limit. See the table at the end of the instructions for Form 2555 for daily and annual limits. If your city is not listed, then you are limited to the standard daily rate listed above.

An exclusion is an adjustment to your gross income. You will report all of your wages or self-employed income, but then subtract the amount you are allowed to exclude, per Form 2555, before calculating your adjusted gross income.

To qualify for the exclusion, you must have earned income that is taxable in the foreign country and meet either the:

- bona fide residence test, or

- physical presence test.

6.1 Bona fide residence test

To meet the test, you must be one of the following:

- a US citizen who is a resident of a foreign country for an entire tax year, or

- a US green card holder who is a citizen or national of a country which has a tax treaty with the US, and who is a resident of that foreign country for the entire tax year.

6.2 Physical presence test

You meet the physical presence test if you are physically present in a foreign country 330 full days during a period of 12 consecutive months. The 330 days do not have to be consecutive. Any US citizen or green card holder can use the physical presence test to qualify for the exclusions and the deduction.

The physical presence test is based only on how long you stay in a foreign country or countries. This test does not depend on the kind of residence you establish, your intentions about returning, or the nature and purpose of your stay abroad.

Generally, to meet the physical presence test, you must be physically present in a foreign country or countries for at least 330 full days during a 12-month period. You can count days you spent abroad for any reason. You do not have to be in a foreign country only for employment purposes, you can be on vacation. A full day is a period of 24 consecutive hours, beginning at midnight.

When you leave the United States to go directly to a foreign country or when you return directly to the United States from a foreign country, the time you spend on or over international waters does not count toward the 330-day total.

6.3 Housing exclusion

The housing exclusion applies only to amounts considered paid for with employer-provided dollars, which includes any amounts paid to you, or paid or incurred on your behalf, by your employer that is taxable foreign earned income to you for the year.

Your housing amount is the total of your housing expenses for the year minus the base housing amount. The computation of the base housing amount is tied to the maximum foreign earned income exclusion. The amount is 16% of the maximum exclusion amount (computed on a daily basis), multiplied by the number of days in your qualifying period that fall within your tax year.

Housing expenses include your reasonable expenses actually paid or incurred for housing in a foreign country for you, your spouse and dependents, if they lived with you. Consider only housing expenses for the part of the year that you qualify for the foreign earned income exclusion.

Housing expenses do not include expenses that are lavish or extravagant, the cost of buying property, purchased furniture or accessories, and improvements and other expenses that increase the value or appreciably prolong the life of your property.

You also cannot include in housing expenses the value of meals or lodging that you exclude from gross income (under the rules for the exclusion of meals and lodging), or that you deduct as moving expenses.

Also, for purposes of determining the foreign housing exclusion or deduction, your housing expenses eligible to be considered in calculating the housing cost amount may not exceed a certain limit. The limit on housing expenses is generally 30% of the maximum foreign earned income exclusion, but it may vary depending upon the location in which you incur housing expenses.

Additionally, foreign housing expenses may not exceed your total foreign earned income for the taxable year. Your foreign housing deduction cannot be more than your foreign earned income less the total of your foreign earned income exclusion, plus your housing exclusion.

Note: Although the foreign housing exclusion and/or the deduction will reduce your regular income tax, they will not reduce your self-employment tax.

7. Owning Real Estate in the US

If you buy US real estate as a resident of Canada, you will likely be required to file and report a "foreign investment in US real estate."

A series of forms that are frequently overlooked are those from the Bureau of Economic Analysis (BEA), a division of the US Department of

Commerce. These forms are typically not completed by advisors because of their obscurity and by the fact that they are not tax forms, accountants generally do not consider it their responsibility.

The BEA produces comprehensive statistics on foreign direct investment in the US. The statistics, which are the world's most comprehensive and accurate, are obtained from mandatory surveys. Even if you are exempt from filing, you are still required to file BE-15 Claim for Exemption, to prove your exemption. In other words, even if you would have been exempt except for the fact you failed to file the Claim for Exemption, you are liable for all of the penalties and possible imprisonment of a person or company that is not exempt.

To be eligible for exemption, your assets, sales, or net income have to be $40 million or less. This makes virtually everyone reading this book exempt, if they file form BE-15 Claim for Exemption. If you are buying the property through an entity, Form BE-605 is required.

If you are buying the property for personal use (e.g., not for a business reason), you are exempt and do not have to file the claim for exemption.

Filing requirements:

- A foreign person (see below)
- Direct or indirect ownership interest of at least 10% of the voting stock, or equivalent
- File electronically at www.bea.gov/efile
- Due June 30

A "foreign person" is defined as anyone that is a resident outside the US and is subject to the jurisdiction of another country. That means that if you are a US citizen or green card holder living in Canada, investing in US real estate, you are required to complete these forms.

The following information is from one of the forms (BE-15) that are required to be completed. Failure to report is subject to a civil penalty of not less than $2,500, and not more than $25,000. The civil penalties are subject to inflationary adjustments. Willfully failing to report can lead to fines of not more than $10,000 and/or imprisonment for not more than one year.

The law provides that your survey is confidential and may be used only for analytical or statistical purposes. The information cannot be presented in a manner that allows it to be individually identified. Your report cannot be used for purposes of taxation, investigation, or regulation. Copies retained by the Bureau are immune from the legal process.

Obviously, with a $40 million threshold, a very large portion of the investors in US real estate will qualify for the exemption. However, you must file to claim the exemption. Consider going to a different advisor if your advisor either is not aware of the BEA forms or is unwilling to prepare them for you.

8. Foreign Trust Rules

Foreign trusts are a very complicated area of law and you would only use experienced cross-border advisors when using or considering to use a trust.

8.1 Canadian foreign trusts

The Canadian Supreme Court ruled that in determining the residency of a trust, you must determine where its real business is carried on, which is where the central management and control of the trust actually takes place (mind and management). The mind and management is typically the trustee, so for example, if you have a US trust with an independent US trustee, the trust would most likely be considered a nonresident trust.

When making a determination as to the jurisdiction in which the central management and control of a trust is exercised, the CRA will consider any relevant factor, which may include:

- the factual role of a trustee and other persons with respect to the trust property, including any decision-making limitations imposed thereon, either directly or indirectly, by any beneficiary, settlor or other relevant person, and

- the ability of a trustee and other persons to select and instruct trust advisors with respect to the overall management of the trust.

For this purpose, the CRA will look to any evidentiary support that demonstrates the exercise of decision-making powers and responsibilities over the trust.

After an examination of all factors, it may be determined that a trust is resident in Canada even if another country considers the trust to be resident in that other country.

8.1a Deemed residency

Trusts that are not factually resident in Canada may be deemed to be resident in Canada for a tax year under the nonresident trust rules in section 94 for certain purposes, including computing the income of the trust and determining its liability for Part I tax. These rules are applicable to a factually non-resident trust (other than an exempt foreign trust) if there is a resident contributor to the trust or a resident beneficiary under the trust. A detailed description of those provisions would be beyond the scope of this chapter.

Generally, each of the resident contributors to a deemed resident trust, and the resident beneficiaries under the trust are jointly and severally liable with the trust for many of its obligations, including its Part I tax liability.

The *Income Tax Conventions Interpretation Act* contains rules that govern the interpretation of certain provisions of the tax treaties negotiated by Canada. Section 4.3 of this act came into force on March 5, 2010 to clarify that under Canadian law, a trust that is deemed to be resident in Canada by subsection 94(3) will be deemed to be a resident of Canada and not a resident of the other contracting state for the purposes of applying a particular tax convention. This will be the case notwithstanding the provisions of the particular convention or of the act giving the convention the force of law in Canada.

If a trust is determined to be deemed resident of Canada it will be subject to Canadian tax. Trusts in Canada are taxed at the highest marginal tax rate (33% federal), plus the highest provincial tax rate. Since a nonresident trust will not be located in a province, at tax equal to 48% of the federal rate, or 15.84%, for a total Canadian tax of 48.84%.

8.2 US foreign trusts

A foreign trust exists unless both of the following conditions are satisfied:

- a court within the US exercises primary supervision over the administration of the trust, and
- one or more US persons have authority to control all substantial decisions of the trust.

These are called the "court" and "control" tests.

Substantial decisions generally means decisions that persons are authorized or required to make under the terms of the trust agreement. Such decisions include, for example, the amount and timing of distributions and whether to make them from income or principal, the selection of beneficiaries, investment decisions, whether to terminate the trust, and decisions regarding trustee changes.

8.3 General rules of trust taxation

There are several regimes for taxing trusts, depending upon whether they are grantor trusts (simple trusts) or complex trusts. In addition, there are several special rules applicable to foreign trusts or trusts having non-US grantors. A grantor of a trust is the person that creates the trust and names the beneficiaries of the trust.

A grantor trust will generally have its income and gains flow through to the grantor and taxed in his or her hands. A trust having a US grantor will be considered a grantor trust if he retains certain interests or powers over the trust property.

Important: A foreign trust established by a US person (citizen or green card holder) that has, or may have, US beneficiaries will also be considered a grantor trust, even if the grantor has retained no interests in or powers over the trust. In addition, a foreign trust established by a non-US person who becomes a US person within five years of transferring property to the trust, directly or indirectly, will be a grantor trust if, at the grantor's residency starting date, the trust has a US beneficiary.

Example: If your parents who are not US persons (citizens, residents, or green card holders), form a Canadian trust and name you (a US person) as a beneficiary, they now have a US grantor trust.

If a trust (whether domestic or foreign) has a grantor that is not a US person, more limited rules apply in determining whether the trust will be treated as a grantor trust. In such a case, a trust generally will be treated as a grantor trust only if it is revocable by the grantor (either alone or with the consent of a related or subordinate party who is subservient to the grantor); or distributions (whether of income or principal) may be made only to the grantor or the grantor's spouse during the grantor's lifetime.

In contrast, a non-grantor trust (whether domestic or foreign) is a separate taxpayer for US federal income tax purposes. A non-grantor trust is generally taxed in the same manner as individuals, with certain modifications. Thus, like a US citizen or resident, a domestic trust will pay US tax on its worldwide income and capital gains. Items of ordinary income (including, for example, rents, royalties, certain dividends and interest) generally are taxed at graduated rates of up to 39.6%, after the allowance of certain deductions and credits. Gains from the sale or exchange of capital assets (such as stock) held for more than 12 months generally are taxed at a long-term capital gain rate of up to 23.8%. Gains arising from the sale or exchange of capital assets held for twelve months or less are generally taxed at the trust's ordinary income tax rate. Like a nonresident alien, a foreign trust will pay US income tax only on its income and certain gains from US sources and on income or gain that is "effectively connected" to a US trade or business.

In calculating its taxable income, a trust will receive a deduction for distributions to its beneficiaries, to the extent that these distributions carry out the trust's Distributable Net Income (DNI) for the taxable year. Any DNI distributed will retain its character in the hands of the recipient beneficiaries and will be taxed to them. In the case of domestic trusts, DNI consists of the trust's fiduciary accounting income, with certain adjustments. Thus, any distributions of DNI by a domestic trust to beneficiaries will constitute ordinary income in their hands and will be taxed at their applicable income tax rate. Capital gains of a domestic trust generally do not enter into the DNI calculation and are usually taxed to the trust. Any distributions by a domestic trust to beneficiaries in excess of DNI will be a nontaxable distribution of capital; thus, any accumulated income and gains of a domestic trust are taxed only to the trust and are not taxed again when distributed to a beneficiary.

Foreign trusts must include both capital gain and ordinary income items in their DNI. Distributions to beneficiaries are considered first to carry out the DNI of the current year (pro rata as to each item of income or gain) and will be taxed to the recipient beneficiaries. The ordinary income portion generally will be taxed to the beneficiaries at their respective graduated income tax rates, while the long-term capital gain portion will be taxed up to the 23.8% capital gains rate.

In order for a trust to obtain a distribution deduction for a transfer of property to another trust, it must be clear that the transfer to the second trust represents a distribution to a "beneficiary." For this purpose, a beneficiary is defined to include "an heir, legatee, or devisee (including an estate or trust)." Thus, it is specifically contemplated that a trust can be a beneficiary and receive distributions of DNI. On the other hand, if the transfer represents only a division of the first trust into sub-trusts, then the second trust will be considered to have received a pro rata portion of each of the first trust's account items, including DNI, UNI, and capital, and there will have been no distribution to a beneficiary that carries out trust income first.

8.4 Throwback rule

The Code contains a number of special taxing provisions applicable to foreign trusts. Perhaps the most important of these, the "throwback rule" applicable to distributions of accumulated income from foreign trusts.

If a foreign trust does not distribute all of its DNI in the current year, the after-tax portion of the undistributed DNI will become Undistributed Net Income (UNI). In subsequent tax years, any distributions from the trust in excess of the DNI of the current taxable year will be considered to come next from UNI, if any, on a first-in, first-out basis. Only after DNI and UNI are exhausted are distributions considered to come from non-taxable trust capital.

Distributions of the UNI of a foreign trust received by a US beneficiary are taxed under the throwback rule, which generally seeks to treat a beneficiary as having received the income in the year in which it was earned by the trust. The throwback rule effectively results in tax being levied at the recipient's highest marginal income tax rate for the year in which the income or gain was earned by the trust. Thus, any capital gains accumulated by a foreign trust for distribution in a later taxable year lose their character and are treated as ordinary income. In addition, the throwback rule adds an interest charge to the taxes on a throwback distribution in order to offset the benefits of tax deferral. The interest charge accrues for the period beginning with the year in which the income or gain is recognized and ending with the year that the UNI amount is distributed, and is assessed at the rate applicable to underpayments of tax, as adjusted, compounded daily.

Because of the draconian consequences of the throwback rule, which can leave little net economic benefit after tax and interest charges when long-accumulated earnings are distributed to US beneficiaries, many foreign trusts having substantial UNI accounts distribute only DNI on a current basis, preferring to maintain their pool of UNI as an untaxed lodestone to earn more current income. Even domesticating a foreign trust in the US, which no longer has a throwback rule for domestic trusts, does not avoid the consequences of the throwback rule. The throwback rule continues to apply to such a trust to the extent that trust distributions following domestication are made from the historic UNI account accumulated while the trust was a foreign trust.

Thus, there is a general desire of foreign trusts (and domesticated foreign trusts) to find a means to access their accumulations without suffering the full economic consequences of the throwback rule. Because, following enactment of the 1996 Small Business Act, Treasury needed to provide guidance for US beneficiaries receiving distributions from foreign trusts accompanied by no information to assist them with the proper reporting of the distribution, Treasury and the Service created the so-called "default method" as a means by which a beneficiary of a foreign trust having no knowledge of the character of receipts from the trust can report his receipts for US tax purposes. An incidental benefit of the default rule is that it allows foreign trusts with UNI accounts to distribute their accumulated earnings to US beneficiaries without causing them to suffer the full economic consequences of the throwback rule, in particular the interest charge for the benefit of deferral. However, there can be some trade-offs in electing to use the default method. Once the default method is used, the actual character of all distributions (except those received in the last year of the trust) will be lost, and all distributions will be taxable at rates applicable to "ordinary income," even if the trust otherwise would be considered to distribute long-term capital gains, tax-exempt income, or even nontaxable trust capital.

Under the default method, only tax on that portion of a foreign trust distribution that exceeds 125% of the average of the distributions received during the prior three years is subject to the compounded interest charge applicable to accumulation distributions. Thus, it should be possible economically to model distributions from a trust to ensure that no amount of a distribution ever exceeds 125% of the prior three-year average distribution. When it comes time to consider how to, effectively, bail out the trust's UNI account, the trustees can employ investment strategies to create sufficient DNI in each year of the three-year averaging periods that will enable them comfortably to distribute the remaining UNI to beneficiaries electing to report their receipts under the default method over the remaining years of the trust. Obviously, this will depend upon the value of the UNI account, the number of trust years remaining, and the trustees' ability to generate sufficient income during the averaging period, among other things.

Once a trust's default distributions have carried out all UNI, the trustees can elect to terminate the trust. In the last year, the trust is once again entitled to use the actual method in determining the tax consequences of the distributions to the beneficiaries. If only capital or other non-taxable items remain (e.g., tax-exempt income), the final year distributions to beneficiaries will be tax-free.

8.5 Transfers to a foreign trust

Any transfer of property by a US person (any US taxpayer) to a foreign trust is treated as a taxable exchange of the property, except in certain circumstances.

The principal exception to the gain recognition rule is for transfers to foreign trusts if any person is treated as owner of the trust under the grantor trust rules. Thus, if you transfer assets to a foreign trust that you created (grantor trust) there is no gain on the transfer.

Generally, if a domestic trust becomes a foreign trust, it is treated as a taxable transfer by the domestic trust of all property to a foreign trust immediately before the trust's change of residence status.

8.6 Loans from foreign trusts; intermediary transfers

Generally, loans of cash or marketable securities by a foreign trust to any grantor, beneficiary or other US person related to a grantor or beneficiary is treated as a trust distribution, and is taxable under the normal trust rules. However, if the loan is made to a person other than a grantor or beneficiary, it will be treated as a distribution to the grantor or beneficiary to whom the person is related.

Note: The repayment of principal or interest of a foreign trust loan treated as a distribution (as described above) is disregarded for tax purposes. This means that the US person cannot deduct interest payments for any tax purpose.

8.7 Tax reporting

The foreign trust reporting rules require disclosure by US persons of the following information pertaining to transactions involving foreign trusts:

1. A responsible party (e.g., grantor, transferor or executor) must provide notice of (i) the creation of a foreign trust by a US person, (ii) the transfer of money or property to a foreign trust, including by reason of death, (iii) the death of a US person treated as owner of a foreign trust under the grantor trust rules or if any portion of a foreign trust was included in the decedent's estate.

2. US persons treated as owners of a foreign trust must annually file a return confirming such status and must also ensure that the trust files a return providing a full and complete accounting of all trust activities and operations and provides an annual statement to the owner and any US person who receives a distribution from the trust.

3. US beneficiaries of a foreign trust who receive any distribution during a taxable year, whether or not taxable, must disclose such receipt. If the disclosure is not accompanied by adequate records to determine the proper tax treatment of the distribution, the IRS is authorized to treat the entire distribution as an accumulation distribution subject to a somewhat modified version of the "throwback rule" previously described.

The reporting of transactions by grantors, transferors, owners and beneficiaries is done on Form 3520. Form 3520, if due from a taxpayer, is required to be filed on or before April 15 for a taxpayer's income tax return. A trust's return on Form 3520-A, is required to be filed on or before March 15 of each year for the preceding year. Extensions can be filed for both forms.

Note: There is a difference in the filing dates of these two forms.

The penalties for failure to file (or not filing on time) the several trust information returns are significant. The penalty for failure to file notice of a transfer in trust or receipt of a trust distribution under is 35% of the gross value of property transferred to the trust or received, respectively. If a US owner of a foreign trust fails to ensure that a trust return is filed on Form 3520-A, the applicable penalty is equal to 5% of the gross value of assets considered owned by the taxpayer at the end of the year in question. Additional penalties of $10,000 USD per month can accrue for continued failure to report after receipt of a notice from the IRS. In all cases, the penalties may be abated if the taxpayer can demonstrate that the failure to timely file a required information return was due to "reasonable cause." The fact that a foreign jurisdiction would impose a civil or criminal penalty for disclosing the information is expressly not considered to be reasonable cause.

Finally, in addition to Forms 3520 and 3520-A, an owner or beneficiary of a foreign trust may be required to disclose their financial interest in or signature authority over foreign financial accounts held by the trust, including bank and brokerage accounts, on Form 114 (FBAR), and/or Form 8938. There are also significant penalties for failure to timely file these forms.

12

Americans in Noncompliance with the IRS

There are two types of Americans in Canada; those who know they are Americans and those who don't. You may be thinking, How would I be an American and not know it? Before we get into the various ways in which you could be an American without knowing it, we need to be clear about what we mean when we use the term "American." An American, as we are using the term, means US citizens (by birth or naturalization) and Lawful Permanent Residents (green card holders).

1. Ways of Becoming a US Citizen

Amendment XIV, Section 1, Clause 1 of the US Constitution directs that all persons born in the US are US citizens. This is the case regardless of the tax or immigration status of a person's parents. This means that even if the child was born while the parents were simply visiting or if they were in the US illegally, the child would be a US citizen due to the fact it was born in the US. A person born outside the US may also be a US citizen at birth if at least one parent is a US citizen and has lived in the US for a period of time.

There are two general ways to obtain citizenship through US citizen parents, one at birth and one after birth but before the age of 18. The term "parents" includes: the genetic father, the genetic mother, and the non-genetic gestational mother, if she is the legal parent at the time of birth under the law of the relevant jurisdiction. If there is any ambiguity around whether you could be American, (as it is sometimes possible to be American and not know it!), see the USCIS website at www.uscis.gov.

2. Reporting of Foreign (Non-US) Bank and Financial Accounts

If you have a financial interest in or signature authority over a foreign financial account, including a bank account, brokerage account, mutual fund, trust, or other type of foreign financial account, exceeding certain thresholds, the Bank Secrecy Act may require you to report the account yearly to the Department of Treasury by electronically filing a Financial Crimes Enforcement Network (FinCEN) 114, Report of Foreign Bank and Financial Accounts (FBAR). This form replaces the old Treasury Form TD F90-22.1 form that was required for years prior to the 2013 tax year.

United States persons (defined below) are required to file an FBAR if:

- the United States person had a financial interest in or signature authority over at least one financial account located outside of the United States; and

- the aggregate value of all foreign financial accounts exceeded $10,000 USD at any time during the calendar year reported.

"United States person" includes US citizens; US residents; entities such as corporations, partnerships, or limited liability companies, created or organized in the United States or under the laws of the United States; and trusts or estates formed under the laws of the United States.

Common exceptions for the following United States persons or foreign financial accounts are:

- Certain foreign financial accounts jointly owned by spouses

- Foreign financial accounts owned by an international financial institution

- Owners and beneficiaries of US Individual Retirement Accounts

- Participants in and beneficiaries of US tax-qualified retirement plans

- Certain individuals with signature authority over, but no financial interest in, a foreign financial account

- Trust beneficiaries (but only if a US person reports the account on an FBAR filed on behalf of the trust)

- Foreign financial accounts maintained on a United States military banking facility

The spouse of an individual who files an FBAR is not required to file a separate FBAR if the following conditions are met: (1) all the financial accounts that the non-filing spouse is required to report are jointly owned with the filing spouse; (2) the filing spouse reports the jointly owned accounts on a timely filed FBAR electronically signed; and (3) the filers have completed and signed Form 114a, Record of Authorization to Electronically File FBARs (maintained with the filers' records). Otherwise, both spouses are required to file separate FBARs, and each spouse must report the entire value of the jointly owned accounts.

2.1 Signature authority

Individuals who have signature authority over, but no financial interest in, a foreign financial account are not required to report the account in the following situations:

1. An officer or employee of a bank that is examined by the Office of the Comptroller of the Currency, the Board of Governors of the Federal Reserve System, the Federal Deposit Insurance Corporation, the Office of Thrift Supervision, or the National Credit Union Administration is not required to report signature authority over a foreign financial account owned or maintained by the bank.

2. An officer or employee of a financial institution that is registered with and examined by the Securities and Exchange Commission or Commodity Futures Trading Commission is not required to report signature authority over a foreign financial account owned or maintained by the financial institution.

3. An officer or employee of an Authorized Service Provider is not required to report signature authority over a foreign financial account that is owned or maintained by an investment company that is registered with the Securities and Exchange Commission. Authorized Service Provider means an entity that is registered with and examined by the Securities and Exchange Commission and provides services to an investment company registered under the Investment Company Act of 1940 (e.g., US mutual fund).

4. An officer or employee of an entity that has a class of equity securities listed (or American depository receipts listed) on any US national securities exchange is not required to report signature authority over a foreign financial account of such entity.

5. An officer or employee of a US subsidiary is not required to report signature authority over a foreign financial account of the subsidiary if its US parent has a class of equity securities listed on any US national securities exchange and the subsidiary is included in a consolidated FBAR report of the US parent.

6. An officer or employee of an entity that has a class of equity securities registered (or American depository receipts in respect of equity securities registered) under section 12(g) of the Securities

Exchange Act is not required to report signature authority over a foreign financial account of such entity.

3. Offshore Voluntary Disclosure Program

The Offshore Voluntary Disclosure Program (OVDP) is a voluntary disclosure program specifically designed for taxpayers with exposure to potential criminal liability and/or substantial civil penalties due to a willful failure to report foreign financial assets and pay all tax due in respect of those assets. OVDP is designed to provide taxpayers with such exposure, protection from criminal liability, and terms for resolving their civil tax and penalty obligations.

3.1 Streamlined filing procedures

The streamlined filing compliance procedures described below are available to taxpayers certifying that their failure to report foreign financial assets and pay all tax due in respect of those assets did not result from willful conduct on their part. The streamlined procedures are designed to provide to taxpayers in such situations:

- a streamlined procedure for filing amended or delinquent returns, and

- terms for resolving their tax and penalty obligations.

These procedures will be available for an indefinite period until otherwise announced.

As reflected below, the streamlined filing procedures that were first offered on September 1, 2012 have been expanded and modified to accommodate a broader group of US taxpayers. Major changes to the streamlined procedures include: (1) extension of eligibility to US taxpayers residing in the United States, (2) elimination of the $1,500 tax threshold, and (3) elimination of the risk assessment process associated with the streamlined filing compliance procedure announced in 2012.

The modified streamlined filing compliance procedures are designed for only individual taxpayers, including estates of individual taxpayers. The streamlined procedures are available to both US individual taxpayers residing outside and within the United States. Descriptions of the specific eligibility requirements for the streamlined procedures for both non-US residents (the "Streamlined Foreign Offshore Procedures") and US residents (the "Streamlined Domestic Offshore Procedures") are set forth below.

Taxpayers using either the Streamlined Foreign Offshore Procedures or the Streamlined Domestic Offshore Procedures will be required to certify, in accordance with the specific instructions set forth below, that the failure to report all income, pay all tax, and submit all required information returns, including FBARs (FinCEN Form 114, previously Form TD F 90-22.1), was due to non-willful conduct.

If the IRS has initiated a civil examination of a taxpayer's returns for any taxable year, regardless of whether the examination relates to undisclosed foreign financial assets, the taxpayer will not be eligible to use the streamlined procedures. Taxpayers under examination may consult with their agent. Similarly, a taxpayer under criminal investigation by IRS Criminal Investigation is also ineligible to use the streamlined procedures.

Taxpayers eligible to use the streamlined procedures who have previously filed delinquent or amended returns in an attempt to address US tax and information reporting obligations with respect to foreign financial assets (so-called "quiet disclosures" made outside of the OVDP or its predecessor programs) may still use the streamlined procedures by following the instructions set forth below. However, any penalty assessments previously made with respect to those filings will not be abated.

All tax returns submitted under the streamlined procedures must have a valid Taxpayer Identification Number (TIN). For US citizens, resident aliens, and certain other individuals, the proper TIN is a valid Social Security Number (SSN). For individuals who are not eligible for an SSN, an Individual Taxpayer Identification Number (ITIN) is a valid TIN. Tax returns submitted without a valid SSN or ITIN will not be processed under the streamlined procedures. However, for taxpayers who are ineligible for an SSN but do not have an ITIN, a submission may be made under the streamlined procedures if accompanied by a complete ITIN application.

Tax returns submitted under either the Streamlined Foreign Offshore Procedures or the Streamlined Domestic Offshore Procedures will be processed like any other return submitted to the IRS. Consequently, receipt of the returns will not be acknowledged by the IRS and the streamlined filing process will not culminate in the signing of a closing agreement with the IRS.

Returns submitted under either the Streamlined Foreign Offshore Procedures or the Streamlined Domestic Offshore Procedures will not be subject to IRS audit automatically, but they may be selected for audit under the existing audit selection processes applicable to any US tax return and may also be subject to verification procedures in that the accuracy and completeness of submissions may be checked against information received from banks, financial advisors, and other sources. Thus, returns submitted under the streamlined procedures may be subject to IRS examination, additional civil penalties, and even criminal liability, if appropriate.

Caution: Taxpayers who are concerned that their failure to report income, pay tax, and submit required information returns was due to willful conduct and who therefore seek assurances that they will not be subject to criminal liability and/or substantial monetary penalties should consider participating in the Offshore Voluntary Disclosure Program and should consult with their professional tax or legal advisers.

After a taxpayer has completed the streamlined filing compliance procedures, he or she will be expected to comply with US law for all future years and file returns according to regular filing procedures.

Once a taxpayer makes a submission under either the Streamlined Foreign Offshore Procedures or the Streamlined Domestic Offshore Procedures, the taxpayer may not participate in OVDP. Similarly, a taxpayer who submits an OVDP voluntary disclosure letter pursuant to OVDP FAQ 24 on or after July 1, 2014, is not eligible to participate in the streamlined procedures.

A taxpayer eligible for treatment under the streamlined procedures who submits, or has submitted, a voluntary disclosure letter under the OVDP (or any predecessor offshore voluntary disclosure program) prior to July 1, 2014, but who does not yet have a fully executed OVDP closing agreement, may request treatment under the applicable penalty terms available under the streamlined procedures. A taxpayer seeking such treatment does not need to opt out of OVDP, but will be required to certify, in accordance with the instructions set forth below, that the failure to report all income, pay all tax, and submit all required information returns, including FBARs, was due to non-willful conduct. As part of the OVDP process, the IRS will consider this request in light of all the facts and circumstances of the taxpayer's case and will determine whether or not to incorporate the streamlined penalty terms in the OVDP closing agreement.

3.2 Eligibility for the streamlined foreign offshore procedures

In addition to having to meet the general eligibility criteria described above, individual US taxpayers, or estates of individual US taxpayers, seeking to use the Streamlined Foreign Offshore Procedures described in this section must: (1) meet the applicable non-residency requirement described below (for joint return filers, both spouses must meet the applicable non-residency requirement described below) and (2) have failed to report the income from a foreign financial asset and pay tax as required by US law, and may have failed to file an FBAR with respect to a foreign financial account, and such failures resulted from non-willful conduct. Non-willful conduct is conduct that is due to negligence, inadvertence, or mistake or conduct that is the result of a good faith misunderstanding of the requirements of the law.

Individual US citizens or Lawful Permanent Residents, or estates of US citizens or Lawful Permanent Residents, meet the applicable non-residency requirement if, in any one or more of the most recent three years for which the US tax return due date (or properly applied-for extended due date) has passed, the individual did not have a US abode and the individual was physically outside the United States for at least 330 full days. Neither temporary presence of the individual in the United States nor maintenance of a dwelling in the United States by an individual necessarily mean that the individual's abode is in the United States.

Example 1

Mr. W was born in the United States but moved to Canada with his parents when he was five years old, has lived there ever since, and does not have a US abode. Mr. W meets the non-residency requirement applicable to individuals who are US citizens or Lawful Permanent Residents.

Example 2

Assume the same facts as Example 1, except that Mr. W moved to the United States and acquired a US abode in 2015. The most recent 3 years for which Mr. W's US tax return due date has passed are 2016, 2015, and 2014. Mr. W meets the non-residency requirement applicable to individuals who are US citizens or Lawful Permanent Residents.

Individuals who are not US citizens or Lawful Permanent Residents, or estates of individuals who were not US citizens or Lawful Permanent Residents, meet the applicable non-residency requirement if, in any one or more of the last three years for which the US tax return due date (or properly applied for extended due date) has passed, the individual did not meet the substantial presence test.

Example 3

Ms. X is not a US citizen or Lawful Permanent Resident, was born in Canada, and resided in Canada until May 1, 2015, when her employer transferred her to the United States. Ms. X was physically present in the US for more than 183 days in both 2015 and 2016. The most recent 3 years for which Ms. X's US tax return due date has passed are 2016, 2015, and 2014. While Ms. X met the substantial presence test for 2015 and 2016, she did not meet the substantial presence test for 2014. Ms. X meets the non-residency requirement applicable to individuals who are not US citizens or Lawful Permanent Residents.

3.3 Scope and effect of procedures

US taxpayers (US citizens, Lawful Permanent Residents, and those meeting the substantial presence test) are eligible to use the Streamlined Foreign Offshore Procedures must:

- for each of the most recent three years for which the US tax return due date has passed, file delinquent or amended tax returns, together with all required information returns (e.g., Forms 3520, 5471, and 8938), and

- for each of the most recent six years for which the FBAR due date has passed, file any delinquent FBARs.

The full amount of the tax and interest due in connection with these filings must be remitted with the delinquent or amended returns.

A taxpayer who is eligible to use these Streamlined Foreign Offshore Procedures and who complies with all of the instructions outlined below will not be subject to failure-to-file and failure-to-pay penalties, accuracy-related penalties, information return penalties, or FBAR penalties. Even if returns properly filed under these procedures are subsequently selected for audit under existing audit selection processes, the taxpayer will not be subject to failure-to-file and failure-to-pay penalties or accuracy-related penalties with respect to amounts reported on those returns, or to information return penalties or FBAR penalties, unless the examination results in a determination that the original tax noncompliance was fraudulent and/or that the FBAR violation was willful. Any previously assessed penalties with respect to those years, however, will not be abated. Further, as with any US tax return filed in the normal course, if the IRS determines an additional tax deficiency for a return submitted under these procedures, the IRS may assert applicable additions to tax and penalties relating to that additional deficiency.

For returns filed under these procedures, retroactive relief will be provided for failure to timely elect income deferral on certain retirement and savings plans where deferral is permitted by the applicable treaty. The proper deferral elections with respect to such plans must be made with the submission. See the instructions below for the information required to be submitted to make such elections.

The risk assessment process associated with the 2012 Streamlined Filing Compliance Procedures for nonresident, non-Filer US taxpayers has been eliminated for all streamlined filers. A taxpayer who has initiated participation in the 2012 Streamlined Filing Compliance Procedures prior to July 1, 2014, and has not already been notified of a high or low risk determination will not receive correspondence related to their risk determination and the returns will be processed without regard to that risk assessment.

3.4 Specific instructions

Failure to follow these instructions or to submit the items described below will result in returns being processed in the normal course without the benefit of the favorable terms of these procedures.

For each of the most recent three years for which the US tax return due date (or properly applied for extended due date) has passed:

- if a US tax return has not been filed previously, submit a complete and accurate delinquent tax return using Form 1040, US Individual Income Tax Return, together with the required information returns (e.g., Forms 3520, 5471, and 8938) even if these information returns would normally be filed separately from the Form 1040 had the taxpayer filed on time, or

- if a US tax return has been filed previously, submit a complete and accurate amended tax return using Form 1040X, amended US Individual Income Tax Return, together with the required information returns (e.g., Forms 3520, 5471, and 8938) even if these information returns would normally be filed separately from the Form 1040 had the taxpayer filed a complete and accurate original return.

Include at the top of the first page of each delinquent or amended tax return and at the top of each information return "Streamlined Foreign Offshore" written in red to indicate that the returns are being submitted under these procedures. This is critical to ensure that your returns are processed through these special procedures.

Complete and sign a statement on the Certification by a US Person Residing Outside of the US certifying that you are eligible for the Streamlined Foreign Offshore Procedures; that all required FBARs have now been filed (see instruction 8 below); and that the failure to file tax returns, report all income, pay all tax, and submit all required information returns, including FBARs, resulted from non-willful conduct. You must submit the original signed statement and you must attach copies of the statement to each tax return and information return being submitted through these procedures. You should not attach copies of the statement to FBARs. Failure to submit this statement, or submission of an incomplete or otherwise deficient statement, will result in returns being processed in the normal course without the benefit of the favorable terms of these procedures.

Submit payment of all tax due as reflected on the tax returns and all applicable statutory interest with respect to each of the late payment amounts. Your taxpayer identification number must be included on your check.

If you are not eligible to have a Social Security Number and do not already have an ITIN, submit an application for an ITIN along with the required tax returns, information returns, and other documents filed under these streamlined procedures.

If you seek relief for failure to timely elect deferral of income from certain retirement or savings plans where deferral is permitted by an applicable treaty, submit:

- a statement requesting an extension of time to make an election to defer income tax and identifying the applicable treaty provision;

- a dated statement signed by you under penalties of perjury describing:

  - the events that led to the failure to make the election,

  - the events that led to the discovery of the failure, and

  - if you relied on a professional advisor, the nature of the advisor's engagement and responsibilities; and

- for relevant Canadian plans, a Form 8891 (Form discontinued) for each tax year and each plan and a description of the type of plan covered by the submission.

- the documents listed above, together with the payments described above, must be sent in paper form (electronic submissions will not be accepted) to:

Internal Revenue Service
3651 South I-H 35
Stop 6063 AUSC
Attn: Streamlined Foreign Offshore
Austin, TX 78741

Note: This address may only be used for returns filed under these procedures. For all future filings, you must file according to regular filing procedures.

For each of the most recent six years for which the FBAR due date has passed, file delinquent FBARs according to the FBAR instructions and include a statement explaining that the FBARs are being filed as part of the Streamlined Filing Compliance Procedures. You are required to file these delinquent FBARs electronically at FinCEN. On the cover page of the electronic form, select "Other" as the reason for filing late. An explanation box will appear. In the explanation box, enter "Streamlined Filing Compliance Procedures."

If you are unable to file electronically, you may contact FinCEN's Regulatory Helpline at 1-800-949-2732 or 1-703-905-3975 (if calling from outside the United States) to determine possible alternatives to electronic filing.

3.5 Eligibility for the streamlined domestic offshore procedures

In addition to having to meet the general eligibility criteria described above, individual US taxpayers, or estates of individual US taxpayers seeking to use the Streamlined Domestic Offshore Procedures must: (1) fail to meet the applicable non-residency requirement (for joint return filers, one or both of the spouses must fail to meet the applicable non-residency requirement); (2) have previously filed a US tax return (if required) for each of the most recent three years for which the US tax return due date (or properly applied for extended due date) has passed; (3) have failed to report gross income from a foreign financial asset and pay tax as required by US law, and may have failed to file an FBAR (FinCEN Form 114, previously Form TD F 90-22.1) and/or one or more international information returns (e.g., Forms 3520, 3520-A, 5471, 5472, 8938, 926, and 8621) with respect to the foreign financial asset, and (4) such failures resulted from non-willful conduct. Non-willful conduct is conduct that is due to negligence, inadvertence, or mistake or conduct that is the result of a good faith misunderstanding of the requirements of the law.

3.6 Scope and effect of procedures

US taxpayers (US citizens, Lawful Permanent Residents, and those meeting the substantial presence test) eligible to use the Streamlined Domestic Offshore Procedures must (1) for each of the most recent three years for which the US tax return due date (or properly applied for extended due date) has passed (the "covered tax return period"), file amended tax returns, together with all required information returns (e.g., Forms 3520, 3520-A, 5471, 5472, 8938, 926, and 8621), (2) for each of the most recent six years for which the FBAR due date has passed (the "covered FBAR period"), file any delinquent FBARs (FinCEN Form 114), and (3) pay the "miscellaneous offshore penalty." The full amount of the tax, interest, and miscellaneous offshore penalty due in connection with these filings should be remitted with the amended tax returns.

The miscellaneous offshore penalty is equal to 5% of the highest aggregate balance/value of the taxpayer's foreign financial assets that are subject to the miscellaneous offshore penalty during the years in the covered tax return period and the covered FBAR period. For this purpose, the highest aggregate balance/value is determined by aggregating the year-end account balances and year-end asset values of all the foreign financial assets subject to the miscellaneous offshore penalty for each of the years in the covered tax return period and the covered FBAR period and selecting the highest aggregate balance/value from among those years.

A foreign financial asset is subject to the 5% miscellaneous offshore penalty in a given year in the covered FBAR period if the asset should have been, but was not, reported on an FBAR (FinCEN Form 114) for that year. A foreign financial asset is subject to the 5% miscellaneous offshore penalty in a given year in the covered tax return period if the asset should have been, but was not, reported on a Form 8938 for that year. A foreign financial asset is also subject to the 5-percent miscellaneous offshore penalty in a given year in the covered tax return period if the asset was properly reported for that year, but gross income in respect of the asset was not reported in that year.

A taxpayer who is eligible to use these Streamlined Domestic Offshore Procedures and who complies with all of the instructions will be subject only to the miscellaneous offshore penalty and will not be subject to accuracy-related penalties, information return penalties, or FBAR penalties. Even if returns properly filed under these procedures are subsequently selected for audit under existing audit selection processes, the taxpayer will not be subject to accuracy-related penalties with respect to amounts reported on those returns, or to information return penalties or FBAR penalties, unless the examination results in a determination that the original return was fraudulent and/or that the FBAR violation was willful. Any previously assessed penalties with respect to those years, however, will not be abated. Further, as with any US tax return filed in the normal course, if the IRS determines an additional tax deficiency for a return submitted under these procedures, the IRS may assert applicable additions to tax and penalties relating to that additional deficiency.

For returns filed under these procedures, retroactive relief will be provided for failure to timely elect income deferral on certain retirement and savings plans where deferral is permitted by the applicable treaty. The proper deferral elections with respect to such plans must be made with the submission. See the instructions below for the information required to be submitted with such requests.

3.7 Specific instructions

Failure to follow these instructions or to submit the items described below will result in returns being processed in the normal course without the benefit of the favorable terms of these procedures.

1. For each of the most recent three years for which the US tax return due date (or properly applied-for extended due date) has passed, submit a complete and accurate amended tax return using Form 1040X, amended US Individual Income Tax Return, together with any required information returns (e.g., Forms 3520, 3520-A, 5471, 5472, 8938, 926, and 8621) even if these information returns would normally not be submitted with the Form 1040 had the taxpayer filed a complete and accurate original return. You may not file delinquent

income tax returns (including Form 1040, US Individual Income Tax Return) using these procedures.

2. Include at the top of the first page of each amended tax return "Streamlined Domestic Offshore" written in red to indicate that the returns are being submitted under these procedures. This is critical to ensure that your returns are processed through these special procedures.

3. Complete and sign a statement on the Certification by US Person Residing in the US certifying: (1) that you are eligible for the Streamlined Domestic Offshore Procedures; (2) that all required FBARs have now been filed; (3) that the failure to report all income, pay all tax, and submit all required information returns, including FBARs, resulted from non-willful conduct; and (4) that the miscellaneous offshore penalty amount is accurate. You must maintain your foreign financial asset information supporting the self-certified miscellaneous offshore penalty computation and be prepared to provide it upon request. You must submit an original signed statement and attach copies of the statement to each tax return and information return being submitted through these procedures. You should not attach copies of the statement to FBARs. Failure to submit this statement, or submission of an incomplete or otherwise deficient statement, will result in returns being processed in the normal course without the benefit of the favorable terms of these procedures.

4. Submit payment of all tax due as reflected on the tax returns and all applicable statutory interest with respect to each of the late payment amounts. Your taxpayer identification number must be included on your check. You may receive a balance due notice or a refund if the tax or interest is not calculated correctly.

5. Submit payment of the miscellaneous offshore penalty as defined above.

6. If you seek relief for failure to timely elect deferral of income from certain retirement or savings plans where deferral is permitted by an applicable treaty, submit:

   - a statement requesting an extension of time to make an election to defer income tax and identifying the applicable treaty provision, and

   - a dated statement signed by you under penalties of perjury describing the events that led to the failure to make the election; the events that led to the discovery of the failure; and if you relied on a professional advisor, the nature of the advisor's engagement and responsibilities.

The documents listed above, together with the payments described above, must be sent in paper form (electronic submissions will not be accepted) to:

Internal Revenue Service
3651 South I-H 35Stop 6063 AUSC
Attn: Streamlined Domestic Offshore
Austin, TX 78741

This address may only be used for returns filed under these procedures. For all future filings, you must file according to regular filing procedures.

For each of the most recent 6 years for which the FBAR due date has passed, file delinquent FBARs according to the FBAR instructions and include a statement explaining that the FBARs are being filed as part of the Streamlined Filing Compliance Procedures. You are required to file these delinquent FBARs electronically at FinCEN. On the cover page of the electronic form, select "Other" as the reason for filing late. An explanation box will appear. In the explanation box, enter "Streamlined Filing Compliance Procedures." If you are unable to file electronically, you may contact FinCEN's Regulatory Helpline at 1-800-949-2732 or 1-703-905-3975 (if calling from outside the US) to determine possible alternatives to electronic filing.

There are two reasons for a taxpayer to enter the IRS' Offshore Voluntary Disclosure Program (OVDP). First, to avoid a criminal prosecution for a willful attempt to evade tax, and the second is to avoid the civil penalty under the Bank Secrecy Act.

A person that is found guilty of willfully evading tax will be guilty of a felony and can spend up to five years in prison and/or fined up to $100,000. To convict someone of willfully evading tax, the government must persuade the judge or jury, beyond a reasonable doubt that there was; (1) an understatement of tax; and (2) willfulness; and (3) at least one affirmative act of evasion. An affirmative act of evasion is any act intended to defraud or deceive the government, such as making a false statement in a tax return or to a federal agent, keeping two sets of books, or dealing only in cash.

The government tends to bring legal charges when a person has schemed for several years and has evaded a substantial amount of tax. In the case of foreign accounts, the amount of tax evaded is not the balance in the accounts, but the much smaller amount of tax on unreported income (interest, dividends, and net capital gains) from the accounts.

The Bank Secrecy Act requires a person with more than $10,000 USD in foreign financial accounts as of December 31 to report the accounts on FinCEN Form 114, Report of Foreign Financial Accounts, (FBAR) by the following June 30. Failure to file an FBAR, that is due, is subject to civil penalty and criminal prosecution. The civil penalty is the greater of $100,000 or 50% of the balance of the account. The civil penalty is only $10,000 if the account owner did not willfully fail to file an FBAR. However, if there is reasonable cause for failing to file an FBAR, there is no penalty at all.

A person convicted willfully failing to file an FBAR is subject to a fine of up to US$100,000, or imprisonment for up to five years, or both.

Under the OVDP, the taxpayer discloses the account(s) and the taxpayer's identity to the IRS Criminal Investigation Division (CID). IRS CID reviews its data base and, if it finds nothing concerning the taxpayer, sends the taxpayer a letter accepting the taxpayer into the OVDP. The letter says that the taxpayer will not be prosecuted concerning the account(s), provided the taxpayer complies with the terms of the OVDP.

The principal terms of the OVDP are:

- the taxpayer must consent to waive the assessment statute of limitations, and file Form 1040X — Amended US Individual Income Tax Return, for the last eight years reporting income on the foreign account(s), and pay the tax due on the Forms 1040X, along with an accuracy-related penalty equal to 20% of the tax, and

- file FBARs for the last eight years, and

- pay a civil penalty, equal to 25% of the highest balance in the account over the last eight years.

Willfulness is a key factor in deciding whether a taxpayer should enter the OVDP. A taxpayer who did not willfully fail to report income from a foreign account would not be subject to criminal tax prosecution concerning the account. And a taxpayer who did not willfully fail to file an FBAR for a foreign account is not subject to the draconian penalty concerning the account.

Willfulness is a voluntary, intentional violation of a known legal duty. A good-faith misunderstanding of the law, whether or not objectively reasonable, negates willfulness. In *United States v. Bishop*, the US Supreme Court observed: "In our complex tax system, uncertainty often arises even among taxpayers who earnestly wish to follow the law. It is not the purpose of the law to penalize frank difference of opinion or innocent errors made despite the exercise of reasonable care." Willfulness must include an evil motive and want of justification in view of all the circumstances.

Misunderstanding or lack of knowledge of the law or facts helps to defend against a finding of willfulness. Complicating the willfulness analysis for taxpayers is that on a schedule to Form 1040 — Schedule B, Interest and Dividends, there are questions in Part III that asks:

- Line 7a "At any time during the tax year, did you have a financial interest in or signature authority over a financial account (such as a bank account, securities account, or brokerage account) located in a foreign country?"

- "If yes, are you required to file FinCEN Form 114, Report of Foreign Bank and Financial Accounts (FBAR), formerly TD F 90-22.1, to report that financial interest or signature authority?"

- Line 7b "If you are required to file FinCEN Form 114, enter the name of the foreign country where the financial account is located."

- Line 8 "During the taxable year, did you receive a distribution from, or were you the grantor of, or transferor to, a foreign trust? If yes, you may have to file Form 3520."

It is difficult for you to claim that you did not know of the requirement to report foreign accounts if you have filed tax returns with "No" checked in the boxes in Schedule B, Line 7a, especially given that you sign the tax return under penalty of perjury. You are less likely to be found willful if the tax return was prepared by a third-party expert, such as a CA or CPA.

Resources

Publications and Useful Readings
Moving to Canada

Welcome to Canada, What You Should Know:
www.cic.gc.ca/english/pdf/pub/welcome.pdf

Start Your Life in Canada:
www.cic.gc.ca/english/newcomers/live

How to Move to Canada:
www.howtomovetocanada.net/disc.htm

Newcomers to Canada
www.cra-arc.gc.ca/E/pub/tg/t4055/t4055-14e.pdf

IRS page on US citizens and green card holders living abroad
www.irs.gov/Individuals/International-Taxpayers/U.S.-Citizens-and-Resident-Aliens-Abroad

Tax Guide for US Citizens and Resident Aliens Abroad
http://www.irs.gov/pub/irs-pdf/p54.pdf

Residency status

Determining Residency Status — Canada:
www.cra-arc.gc.ca/tx/nnrsdnts/cmmn/rsdncy-eng.html

Determining an Individual's Residence Status in Canada —
Tax Folio S5-F1-C1:
www.cra-arc.gc.ca/tx/tchncl/ncmtx/fls/s5/f1/s5-f1-c1-eng.html

Other

Canada Border Services Agency Publications
http://cbsa-asfc.gc.ca/publications/menu-eng.html

US-Canada Agreement on Social Security
https://www.socialsecurity.gov/international/Agreement_Texts/canada.html

Income taxes

Canada — United States Tax Convention Act, 1984
http://laws-lois.justice.gc.ca/eng/acts/C-10.7/FullText.html

IRS Inflation Adjusted numbers for 2016 tax years
https://www.irs.gov/pub/irs-drop/rp-15-53.pdf

IRS taxation of green card holders living abroad
www.irs.gov/pub/irs-wd/14-0033.pdf

Canadian Income Tax Folios
www.cra-arc.gc.ca/tx/tchncl/ncmtx/fls/menu-eng.html

CRA Guides and Pamphlets
www.cra-arc.gc.ca/menu/TGTG_T-e.html

Where to file your US tax return or form
www.irs.gov/uac/Where-to-File-Tax-Returns---Addresses-Listed-by-Return-Type

Useful websites

Canada Revenue Agency
www.cra-arc.gc.ca

Service Canada Offices
www.servicecanada.gc.ca/cgi-bin/sc-srch.cgi?app=hme&ln=eng

Internal Revenue Service
www.irs.gov

Taxpayer Identification Numbers
www.irs.gov/Individuals/International-Taxpayers/Taxpayer-Identification-Numbers-TIN

CRA dispute resolution
http://www.cra-arc.gc.ca/E/pub/tg/p148/p148-11e.pdf

Handy Form Names and Links
IRS forms

114 — Report of Foreign Bank and Financial Accounts (FBAR) — electronic file only
http://bsaefiling.fincen.treas.gov/NoRegFilePDFIndividualFBAR.html

114a — Record of Authorization to Electronically File FBARs
http://bsaefiling.fincen.treas.gov/NoRegFilePDFIndividualFBAR.html

706 — United States Estate (and Generation-Skipping Transfer) Tax Return
https://www.irs.gov/pub/irs-pdf/f706.pdf

709 — United States Gift (and Generation-Skipping Transfer) Tax Return
https://www.irs.gov/pub/irs-pdf/f709.pdf

1040 — US Individual Income Tax Return
https://www.irs.gov/pub/irs-pdf/f1040.pdf

1040-C — US Departing Alien Income Tax Return
https://www.irs.gov/pub/irs-pdf/f1040c.pdf

1040NR — US Nonresident Alien Income Tax Return
https://www.irs.gov/pub/irs-pdf/f1040nr.pdf

1040X — Amended US Individual Income Tax Return
https://www.irs.gov/pub/irs-pdf/f1040x.pdf

1042 — Annual Withholding Tax Return for US Source Income of
Foreign Persons
https://www.irs.gov/pub/irs-pdf/f1042.pdf

1042-S — Foreign Person's US Source Income Subject to Withholding
https://www.irs.gov/pub/irs-pdf/f1042s.pdf

1116 — Foreign Tax Credit (Individual, Estate or Trust)
https://www.irs.gov/pub/irs-pdf/f1116.pdf

2063 — U.S. Departing Alien Income Tax Statement
https://www.irs.gov/pub/irs-pdf/f2063.pdf

2350 — Application for Extension of Time to File US Income Tax Return
https://www.irs.gov/pub/irs-pdf/f2350.pdf

2555 — Foreign Earned Income
https://www.irs.gov/pub/irs-pdf/f2555.pdf

3520 — Annual Return to Report Transactions with Foreign Trusts and
Receipt of Certain Foreign Gifts
https://www.irs.gov/pub/irs-pdf/f3520.pdf

3520-A — Annual Information Return of Foreign Trust With a US Owner
https://www.irs.gov/pub/irs-pdf/f3520a.pdf

4868 — Application for automatic Extension of Time to File US Individual
Income Tax Return
https://www.irs.gov/pub/irs-pdf/f4868.pdf

5471 — Information Return of US Person with Respect to Certain
Foreign Corporations
https://www.irs.gov/pub/irs-pdf/f5471.pdf

8621 — Information Return by a Shareholder of a Passive Foreign Investment Company or Qualified Electing Fund
https://www.irs.gov/pub/irs-pdf/f8621.pdf

8822 — Change of Address
https://www.irs.gov/pub/irs-pdf/f8822.pdf

8833 — Treaty-Based Return Position Disclosure
https://www.irs.gov/pub/irs-pdf/f8833.pdf

8840 — Closer Connection Exception Statement for Aliens
https://www.irs.gov/pub/irs-pdf/f8840.pdf

8843 — Statement for Exempt Individuals and Individuals with a Medical Condition
https://www.irs.gov/pub/irs-pdf/f8843.pdf

8453 — US Individual Income Tax Transmittal for IRS e-file Return
https://www.irs.gov/pub/irs-pdf/f8453.pdf

8854 — Initial and Annual Expatriation Statement
https://www.irs.gov/pub/irs-pdf/f8854.pdf

8865 — Return of US Persons with Respect to Certain Foreign Partnerships
https://www.irs.gov/pub/irs-pdf/f8865.pdf

8938 — Statement of Specified Foreign Financial Assets
https://www.irs.gov/pub/irs-pdf/f8938.pdf

8960 — Net Investment Income Tax - Individuals, Estate and Trusts
https://www.irs.gov/pub/irs-pdf/f8960.pdf

I-407 — Record of Abandonment of Lawful Resident Status
www.uscis.gov/sites/default/files/files/form/i-407.pdf

W-7 — Application for IRS Individual Taxpayer Identification Number
https://www.irs.gov/pub/irs-pdf/fw7.pdf

W-8BEN — Certificate of Foreign Status of Beneficial Owner for US Tax Withholding and Reporting (Individuals)
https://www.irs.gov/pub/irs-pdf/fw8ben.pdf

W-8CE — Notice of Expatriation and Waiver of Treaty Benefits
www.irs.gov/pub/irs-pdf/fw8ce.pdf

W-8ECI — Certificate of Foreign Person's Claim for Exemption From Withholding on Income Effectively Connected With the Conduct of a Trade or Business in the U.S.
https://www.irs.gov/pub/irs-pdf/fw8eci.pdf

W-9 — Request for Taxpayer Identification Number and Certification (Business Entities)
https://www.irs.gov/pub/irs-pdf/fw9.pdf

CRA forms

NR4 — Statement of Amounts Paid to Credited to Non-Residents of Canada
www.cra-arc.gc.ca/E/pbg/tf/nr4/nr4-15e.pdf

NR6 — Undertaking to File an Income Tax Return by a Non-Resident
Receiving Rent from Real or Immovable Property
www.cra-arc.gc.ca/E/pbg/tf/nr6/nr6-13e.pdf

NR73 — Determination of Residency Status (Leaving Canada)
www.cra-arc.gc.ca/E/pbg/tf/nr73/nr73-12e.pdf

NR74 — Determination of Residency Status (Entering Canada)
www.cra-arc.gc.ca/E/pbg/tf/nr74/nr74-12e.pdf

NR301 — Declaration of eligibility for benefits (reduced tax) under
a tax treaty for a non-resident person
www.cra-arc.gc.ca/E/pbg/tf/nr301/nr301-13e.pdf

NR302 — Declaration of eligibility for benefits (reduced tax) under
a tax treaty for a partnership with non-resident partners
www.cra-arc.gc.ca/E/pbg/tf/nr302/nr302-13e.pdf

NR303 — Declaration of eligibility for benefits (reduced tax) under
a tax treaty for a hybrid entity
www.cra-arc.gc.ca/E/pbg/tf/nr303/nr303-13e.pdf

RC325 — Address change request
www.cra-arc.gc.ca/E/pbg/tf/rc325/rc325-15e.pdf

RC151 — GST/HST Credit Application for Individuals Who Become
Residents of Canada
www.cra-arc.gc.ca/E/pbg/gf/rc151/rc151-15e.pdf

T1 — General — Schedule 1 (Personal Income Tax Return)
www.cra-arc.gc.ca/E/pbg/tf/5000-s1/5000-s1-14e.pdf

T1 — Adjustment Request
www.cra-arc.gc.ca/E/pbg/tf/t1-adj/t1-adj-15e.pdf

T2 — Corporate Income Tax Return
www.cra-arc.gc.ca/E/pbg/tf/t2/t2-15e.pdf

T691 — Alternative Minimum Tax
www.cra-arc.gc.ca/E/pbg/tf/t691/t691-14e.pdf

T1134 — Information Return Relating to Controlled and
Not-Controlled Foreign Affiliates
www.cra-arc.gc.ca/E/pbg/tf/t1134/t1134-12e.pdf

T1135 — Foreign Income Verification Statement
www.cra-arc.gc.ca/E/pbg/tf/t1135/t1135-15e.pdf

T1141 — Information Return In Respect of Transfers or Loans to a Non-Resident Trust
www.cra-arc.gc.ca/E/pbg/tf/t1141/t1141-14e.pdf

T1142 — Information Return in Respect of Distributions from and Indebtedness to a Non-Resident Trust
www.cra-arc.gc.ca/E/pbg/tf/t1142/t1142-fill-10e.pdf

T2036 — Provincial or Territorial Foreign Tax Credit
www.cra-arc.gc.ca/E/pbg/tf/t2036/t2036-fill-14e.pdf

T2057 — Election to Defer the Payment of Income Tax by a Deceased Taxpayer's Legal Representative or Trustee
www.cra-arc.gc.ca/E/pbg/tf/t2057/t2057-14e.pdf

T2125 — Statement of Business or Professional Activities
www.cra-arc.gc.ca/E/pbg/tf/t2125/t2125-14e.pdf

T2209 — Federal Foreign Tax Credits
www.cra-arc.gc.ca/E/pbg/tf/t2209/t2209-fill-14e.pdf

T5013 — Statement of Partnership Income
www.cra-arc.gc.ca/E/pbg/tf/t5013/t5013-15e.pdf

Canadian Health Insurance

Visit your provincial or territorial website for details about health insurance card application procedures:

Alberta:
www.health.alberta.ca/AHCIP/register-for-AHCIP.html

British Columbia:
www2.gov.bc.ca/gov/content/health/health-drug-coverage/msp/bc-residents

Manitoba:
www.gov.mb.ca/health/mhsip/index.html#Q2

New Brunswick:
www2.gnb.ca/content/gnb/en/departments/health/Medicare PrescriptionDrugPlan.html

Newfoundland and Labrador:
www.health.gov.nl.ca/health/mcp/index.html

Northwest Territories:
www.hss.gov.nt.ca/health/nwt-health-care-plan

Nova Scotia:
novascotia.ca/DHW/msi/eligibility.asp

Nunavut:
www.gov.nu.ca/health/information/health-care-card

Ontario:
www.health.gov.on.ca/en/public/programs/ohip/default.aspx

Prince Edward Island:
www.healthpei.ca/healthcard

Quebec:
www.ramq.gouv.qc.ca/en/citizens/health-insurance/registration/Pages/
eligibility.aspx

Saskatchewan:
www.ehealthsask.ca/HealthRegistries/Pages/default.aspx

Yukon:
www.hss.gov.yk.ca/yhcip.php